P9-DFI-911

PREACHING IN A REVOLUTIONARY AGE

BOOKS BY G. BROMLEY OXNAM

PREACHING IN A REVOLUTIONARY AGE

FACING THE FUTURE UNAFRAID

BEHOLD THY MOTHER

BY THIS SIGN CONQUER

THE ETHICAL IDEALS OF JESUS IN A CHANGING WORLD

SOCIAL PRINCIPLES OF JESUS

RUSSIAN IMPRESSIONS

YOUTH AND THE NEW AMERICA

As Editor

EFFECTIVE PREACHING

CREATIVE PREACHING

CONTEMPORARY PREACHING

VARIETIES OF PRESENT-DAY PREACHING

PREACHING AND THE SOCIAL CRISIS

PREACHING IN A REVOLUTIONARY AGE

G. BROMLEY OXNAM

A Bishop of The Methodist Church

ABINGDON-COKESBURY PRESS

New York • *Nashville*

PREACHING IN A REVOLUTIONARY AGE

Wartime Books

Wartime shortage of pulp, manpower, and transportation has produced a severe shortage of paper. In compliance with orders of the War Production Board, wartime books are printed on lighter-weight paper. This reduces thickness and weight. New books have more words to the page and smaller margins. This reduces the number of pages without reducing reading content.

Thinner books save paper, critical copper, and other metals. They help also to avoid wartime increases in book prices. Wartime books appear to be smaller, but their content has not been cut. They are complete. The only change is in appearance.

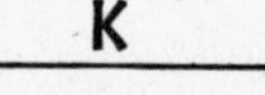

PRINTED IN THE UNITED STATES OF AMERICA

To the Memory of My Father

THOMAS HENRY OXNAM
1854-1915

"He was notable as an engineer, and ever more notable as a man. He was a distinguished mining engineer and a noted preacher."—*The Mining World and Engineering Record,* London, March 20, 1915.

FOREWORD

"A revolution," wrote Prince Kropotkin, "must from its inception be an act of justice to the ill-treated and the oppressed, and not a promise to perform this act of reparation later on. If not, it is sure to fail." [1]

Revolution is a period of action in which faith must become works. A common faith must become a common purpose resulting in a common act. If there can be general agreement upon the question of ends, violence may be avoided when considering the question of means. Failure to unite in a common faith means conflict, because respect for law passes when large sections of the community no longer believe the law to be expressive of the common desire. The unity that results from fear of an enemy seldom lasts long after the enemy is defeated. What we fight for is as important as what we fight. That is a question that involves reasonable agreement in the realm of values. It is because there is insufficient agreement upon the end to be achieved that there is grave danger the present war of the nations may become tomorrow's war of the classes.

If a faith is to unite men who are resolved to create a better society, it must be a faith the people believe to be realizable. To proclaim that the Kingdom of God is unrealizable upon the earth is to turn the masses from the Master to the

1 Quoted by Harold J. Laski in an article in *The Nation,* March 22, 1941.

lesser leaders who not only envision a society of justice and brotherhood but who believe such a society can be created in history. The preacher of the gospel must not identify the absolute of his "good news" with the proposed measures possible in the present hour, but he must be certain that he does not in effect repudiate his faith by relegating its realization to another world.

Men are seeking faith as blind men search for light, but the faith they seek must be one that commands their utter allegiance and promises to satisfy their needs of mind and soul and body here and now. The Christian believes the requisite faith lies in the life and teaching of Jesus. He was and is the Light. The will of God revealed in him is for the Christian the moral law of the universe, and that law must be obeyed if man is to find freedom. Obedience is an act. Men are in no mood to accept "a promise to perform this act of reparation later on." Brotherhood must come alive in the conduct and social practices that express it. So, too, justice. This cannot be done if the relations of men are those that emerge from the practices of selfishness. It was not enlightened self-interest upon which Jesus relied to unite and emancipate man. It was the good will that flows from love. The peoples of the world are about to choose between the weapons of conflict and the tools of co-operation. There is yet time in some lands for change by consent. In others the fateful hour is passed, and the change will be coercive in nature.

In many lands the Church has a compelling voice. It must be Christ's voice. It must affirm the faith, create the purpose, inspire the act. Moreover, the act must reconcile the interests of the one and the many. Such an act depends upon the acceptance and practice of a principle, namely, that the self is truly realized in the complete gift of self for others. The principle demands the fullest development of the self for the good reason that the greater the self becomes, the greater the giving will be. It calls for allegiance to the revolutionary Christ whose way and truth and life were not of violence but of love. It was he who revealed the fact of a loving and just Father of all mankind and thereby lifted man to worth as a son of God and a brother of all men. It was he who compassed religion in the simple command: "Thou shalt love the Lord thy God with all thy heart, and with all thy soul, and with all thy strength, and with all thy mind; and thy neighbor as thyself." He knew that the truth frees, and summoned men to its never-ending pursuit. The preacher who is faithful to him is a called messenger whose profession, with its life and message, becomes socially so necessary in a revolutionary hour that it may, with complete justification, be called sacred.

These lines are written on Easter Sunday afternoon. The churches have been filled with worshipers, and the message of the Risen Lord has been preached. Man seeks assurance of immortality as never before. Millions are to give up their transitory lives before their allotted time. In *The Complete Life* John Erskine quotes from Sénancour's *Obermann* as follows: "It may be that after this life we shall perish utterly, but if that is our fate, let us so live that annihilation will be unjust." The preacher in a revolutionary age who is loyal to Christ will never be plagued by Sénancour's pessimism because in his mind there is no doubt when he proudly and reverently declares, "I believe in . . . the life everlasting." In such a period he will be called upon to read to unnumbered sufferers the consoling words, "Let not your heart be troubled: ye believe in God, believe also in me." But he dare not allow his faith in immortality to become, by indirection, the counsel of an action-destroying otherworldliness. The fact that man is immortal means that man must create a life worthy of an immortal being for that part of his immortality called mortal. A courageous and inspired preaching force, so passionate and so intelligent that it can win the hearts and minds of our generation, may prove to be the body of men who will lead the people to the Promised Land by the splendid roads of peaceful co-operation, and thereby save them from the blood-stained ways of violence.

To Dean Luther A. Weigle, distinguished leader among the religious forces of the nation and former president of the Federal Council of the Churches of Christ in America, who extended the invitation to deliver the Lyman Beecher Lectures of 1944; to Dean Charles R. Brown, inspiring teacher and preacher whose life and work have revealed the preacher at his best; to the faculty and the students of the Divinity School of Yale University, I record my deepest gratitude for the high privilege and honor of having been invited to deliver the Beecher Lectures.

G. Bromley Oxnam

CONTENTS

CHAPTER I

THE REVOLUTIONARY ERA

We stood for a moment before the famous door. Hanging from its sturdy support, a large circular knocker awaited a courageous hand. Above it was the highly polished number "10"; below it, the knob of the door. Before we could knock, the door was opened; and Arthur Henderson, then foreign minister of England, stepped out and walked briskly to a near-by taxi. We entered the hall, hung our hats and coats, and were ushered to a doorway leading to the Cabinet Room. The year was 1934; and Prime Minister J. Ramsay MacDonald, standing just inside the Cabinet Room entrance, greeted his visitors with unmistakable warmth. We sat at the long, green-covered table in the center of the room where the cabinet ministers of Britain had reached decisions and issued ultimatums. Bookcases lined the walls. The windows looked out to a garden and to the Horse Guards parade grounds.

Mr. MacDonald stood beside the prime minister's chair and spoke quietly but fervently, pleading for "greater unity in diversity." "Do not imitate us," he said. "Do not let us imitate you. Let us be different, but one. We ought to differ in measures, but we must be one in spirit." I sat in that Room of Decision taking notes; but my mind took me back to that fateful night of August 4, 1914, when another prime minister with some members of his cabinet waited for the eleven o'clock hour and the reply from Germany to the British ultimatum—a reply they knew would not come but which they prayed for nonetheless.

Asquith was prime minister. He wrote:

> We had an interesting Cabinet, as we got news that the Germans had entered Belgium and had announced that if necessary they would push their way through by force of arms. This simplifies matters. So we sent the Germans an ultimatum to expire at midnight requesting them to give a like assurance with the French that they would respect Belgian neutrality. They have invented a story that the French were meditating an invasion of Belgium and that they were only acting in self-defense, a manifest and transparent lie. Winston, who has got on all his war-paint, is longing for a sea fight in the early hours of the morning to result in the sinking of the *Goeben*. The whole thing fills me with sadness. The House took the fresh news to-day very calmly and with a good deal of dignity, and we got through all the business by half-past four.[1]

Men react differently in the face of great crisis or supreme peril.

Sir Edward Grey, as he was known then, wrote:

> An ultimatum was sent to Berlin. . . . That evening some of us sat with the Prime Minister in the Cabinet Room in 10 Downing Street. I was there in touch with the Foreign Office to certify that no satisfactory reply had come from Berlin, though this was, after all that had happened, a foregone conclusion and a matter of form. Churchill was among those present, ready at

[1] *Memories and Reflections 1852-1927* (Boston: Little, Brown, and Co., 1928), II, 25-26.

the appointed hour to send out the war order, that the fleet were expecting. Midnight came. We were at war.[2]

Asquith is filled with sadness. Grey calmly faces fact and duty. How different is the description by the volatile, the dramatic, the extraordinary David Lloyd George:

> The fourth of August, 1914, is one of the world's fateful dates. The decision taken on that day in the name and on behalf of the British Empire altered the design of Europe. It is not too much to say that it gave a different turn or direction to the advance of the human race. The trumpets of war had already sounded in the East and in the West, and colossal armies were hurrying to the slaughter. Millions of men were either on the march or strapping on their armour for the conflict, and roads and railway tracks trembled with the weight of guns and munitions and all the sinister devices . . . of human destruction!
>
> . . . .
>
> It was a day full of rumours and reports, throbbing with anxiety. . . . The evening came. Still no answer. . . . I was summoned to the Cabinet Room. . . . We sat at the green table in the famous room where so many historic decisions had been taken in the past. . . . In the dimness you might imagine the shades of the great British statesmen of the past taking part in a conference which meant so much to the Empire, to the building up of which they had devoted their lives. . . . In that simple, unadorned, almost dingy room they also had pondered over the problems which had perplexed their day. But never had they been confronted with so tremendous a decision. . . . The ultimatum expired at midnight in Berlin. That was midnight according to Central Europe time: it meant eleven o'clock according to Greenwich time. . . . As the hour approached a deep and tense solemnity fell on the room. . . . Our eyes wandered anxiously from the clock to the door, and from the door to the clock, and little was said. "Boom!" The deep notes of Big Ben rang out

[2] *Twenty-five Years 1892-1916* (New York: Frederick A. Stokes Co., 1925), II, 18.

> into the night. . . . A shuddering silence fell upon the room. Every face was suddenly contracted in a painful intensity. "Doom!" "Doom!" "Doom!" to the last stroke. The big clock echoed in our ears like the hammer of destiny. What destiny? [3]

David Lloyd George mentions that Winston Churchill came in at twenty minutes past the hour. Churchill himself writes:

> It was 11 o'clock at night—12 by German time—when the ultimatum expired. The windows of the Admiralty were thrown wide open in the warm night air. Under the roof from which Nelson had received his orders were gathered a small group of Admirals and Captains and a cluster of clerks, pencil in hand, waiting. Along the Mall from the direction of the Palace the sound of an immense concourse singing "God save the King" floated in. On this deep wave there broke the chimes of Big Ben; and, as the first stroke of the hour boomed out, a rustle of movement swept across the room. The war telegram, which meant "Commence hostilities against Germany," was flashed to the ships and establishments under the White Ensign all over the world.
>
> I walked across the Horse Guards' Parade to the Cabinet room and reported to the Prime Minister and the Ministers who were assembled that the deed was done.[4]

Lloyd George saw tragedy, Churchill beheld glory.

Sadness, duty, tragedy, glory! The world was at war.

I

History also announces ultimatums.

Like the leaders of Britain who awaited the German an-

[3] *War Memoirs of David Lloyd George, 1914-1915* (Boston: Little, Brown, and Co., 1933), pp. 65, 69-72.

[4] *The World Crisis* (New York: Charles Scribner's Sons, 1923), p. 245.

swer on that terrible August night, mankind in revolutionary eras yearns for the reply of reconciliation in the full knowledge that, as the hours become minutes and the minutes become seconds, the dreadful moment of decision arrives. The first thundering stroke of Big Ben, which heretofore had announced the passing hour, spoke of war—and, before its reverberations were still, came the answering thunders of the guns. Repeatedly in history the hours of decision come. Man violates the moral law at his peril. Penalty is exacted. It is the judgment of God.

In such an hour the preacher must proclaim, "Choose you this day whom ye will serve." If he fails, the very stones will cry out. Historic situations emerge in which choice can no longer be postponed. The message must be one of awful clarity and insistent promise. Convictions must become conduct, the Word must become flesh, the ideal must become actuality.

When the police captain whispered to the aged Polycarp, "But what harm is it to say 'Lord Caesar' and to offer sacrifice . . . and be saved?" the old man replied, "If you vainly suppose that I will swear by the genius of Caesar, as you say . . . listen plainly: I am a Christian." John Huss stood in the flames and cried out, "The Lord have mercy!" And Martin Luther concluded, "I can do no other." They knew that One had gone before them. He preached a Sermon on the Mountain. He washed the feet of his disciples in the Upper Room. He offered a prayer of decision in the Garden. But he *gave* his life upon the cross.

Revolution is a cup that must be drunk. It is but human to pray that this may pass from us. It is divine to pray, "Nevertheless not as I will, but as thou wilt." When at last the violations of the moral law have become flagrant and extensive, history speaks in the voice of judgment; the penalty is the tragic suffering of revolution, and darkness falls upon just and unjust alike. What of preaching in such an hour?

Comfortable speech has its proper place, but the hour came when even the Son of Man declared, "Ye serpents, ye generation of vipers, how can ye escape the damnation of hell?" The counsel of winsomeness can be overdone. There is also drawing power in the broken body lifted high upon a cross. Stubbornness, an unattractive trait, may itself become hallowed: he set his face toward Jerusalem. That face did not bear the pleasing smile of One who was all things to all men. Those set lips were soon to phrase the last words of a Man who in agony hung from the cross. "And I, *if I be lifted up from the earth,* will draw all men unto me." *The power of a great memory is often greater than the influence of one who dwells among us, having refused to die for us.*

Reference to committee for further consideration may take certain questions from the floor of history at certain periods, but a motion to postpone in revolutionary eras may be to adjourn sine die. A Roman Catholic sister, highly educated and devoted, justifies the convent life on the ground that in such life discoveries essential to all life are made—discoveries denied to all save those who pay the price of sacrificial separation from the world and in solitude find the secrets of the spirit. Yes, God does speak. Wonders are performed. It is not to deny the fact of revelation to call upon the recipient to act upon the truth revealed. Revolution is a period of action in which men demand means to achieve ends. If those who proclaim the moral ideal do not move from proclamation to measures, revolutionary man is likely to discount the validity of the ideal itself.

There is a selective service act in the realm of religion, and the summons goes out from the King of kings. Training camps do not prepare men for a standing army. The soldiers of the *salons* who have never crossed the threshold that leads to action are forced to choose between the ways of war and the discussion called disinterested. No longer can men sit by the comfortable fireside of contemporary practice, discussing the latest advances in meteorology while men struggle against the blizzard outside. Shoving the toes deep into warm house-slippers, cynically remarking that after all the climate, like human nature, cannot be changed, will not do. Men must act upon their faith. Preaching in a revolutionary era must so reach the mind and heart that the will is stirred and men move out with wills set unflinchingly to do right, ready to submit their faith to the test of the individual it can create and the society it can organize.

It was an impatient parson who insisted that where the trumpet is needed the flute will not suffice and who added that the flute, he feared, was the dominant instrument in the orchestra of organized Christianity. It is not to agree with Dick Sheppard to quote him, but it is important to note the associations of trumpet and flute. The flute calls forth the ballroom, costly raiment, the minuet. The trumpet summons to battlefield, khaki, and the march. Preaching in days of basic change must reject the soft-spoken trivialities of the minuet. It is not the hour for ecclesiastics to gaze in full-length mirrors to be certain episcopal prerogatives are on straight, or to trouble over who will lead the Grand March, or to dance with a bewitching little creature—Mademoiselle

Tactfulness—successfully essaying the crowded floor and avoiding every baffling issue. The minuet precedes revolutions. It is the march that takes precedence in revolutions.

For good or ill, the day of march is upon us; but not all men sing "Lead On, O King Eternal." Some prefer the maintenance of the minuet, its silken garments and graceful bows. The deluge may come later; but for the day let us eat, drink, and be merry. And some are resolved to meet the marchers at the city gates, to defend their privileges house by house, stock certificate by stock certificate. Others take refuge in the sanctuary of the absolute, refusing to touch the relative measure that is less than the ideal, lest they be defiled.

But to be done with figures of speech. It is a revolutionary age.

China seeks in a single generation to appropriate the changes of centuries, and since 1911 has been in a revolution at once political and social, economic and intellectual.

Russia rebelled against the tyranny of Czarist autocracy; the workers in the factories—exploited, congested, easily organized and convinced they were the rightful leaders of the inarticulate peasants—faced an owning group of foreign capitalists who were weak politically because, coming at the invitation of a Russia desiring industrialization, they got what they wanted from government without becoming strong. And back of it all were smouldering fires of resentment in the hearts of the land-hungry peasants. The war of 1914-18 came, and corruption and inefficiency sent thousands to their death. Love of Mother Russia was not deep enough then, for the mother had failed her children. Soldiers threw down their arms. The cries of "Peace" and "Bread" and "Land" arose. And Russia entered revolution.

A defeated Germany turned for a moment to democracy. The victorious Allies turned to revenge. A sinister figure arose, and the people rose to follow. It is scarcely credible that an obscure corporal could leave the battle front in 1918, without money, without health, without higher education, and fifteen years later could stand in the Garrison Church in Potsdam, master of the German people and allegiant to a revolutionary philosophy that is the utter repudiation of Christian faith and political democracy. Germany had become a revolutionary force.

Before Adolph Hitler had done more than attempt a few speeches, Benito Mussolini had marched on Rome, scoffed at liberty, and given his assent to the proposition: "Anti-individualistic, the fascist concept is through the state; and it is for the individual so far as he coincides with the state. . . . For fascism everything is in the state, and nothing, human or spiritual, exists and still less has value outside the state. . . . Fascism believes in neither the possibility nor the utility of perpetual peace."

The so-called March on Rome marked the beginning of the march of fascism, and the end is not yet. It is not necessary to call the roll—Mexico, Spain—and what of India? It is a revolutionary age.

Into this revolutionary era the preacher willy-nilly has been catapulted. What is his role? What is his message? Is he to be the chaplain of the privileged, speaking comfortably to his parishioners—or a court jester laughing away fear? Is he the voice of judgment crying, "Thou art the man," and declaring, "Ye have sold the needy for a pair of shoes"? Should he withdraw from the struggle and conserve the life of the spirit? Or should he be content to bind up the wounds of warriors, to play the role of Good Samaritan? And from whom will he get the pence to pay for the room of the robbed? The preacher in a revolutionary age must speak the changeless Word to a changing world and be ready to give his life for the change necessary to bring contemporary life into harmony with the changeless. He must proclaim the larger loyalties, in which unity lies, to men who seek unity in the lesser loyalties of class and race and nation; and in the persecution that may follow the proclamation he must be ready to forgive men who know not what they do. Upon his lips must be the words of eternal life, the living words of the Lord—also the words of judgment, "Woe unto you, scribes and Pharisees," because he is prophet as well as teacher. If his Father's house is to be a house of prayer, he must speak with whipcords when it is a den of thieves. His ministry cannot be to a class; it is to every child of God.

Thus our Lord suffers the little children to come unto him but speaks against the exploitation of children everywhere; forgives the woman of the streets, charges the sinless to cast the first stone, and then in silence speaks for the unfortunate as never man spake; consoles those whose brother has died and whispers to the ages, "Let not your heart be troubled"; calls a grafter to repentance and checks the sincerity of the repentance by the restoration that follows—a ministry to all, for all, but a ministry that moves from precept to practice, never content until the common life shall be brought into harmony with the moral law, which for him is the will of God.

II

Fear is present in revolution. Fear precedes revolution. Fear is a factor in creating revolution. The privileged fear they will lose their privileges; the underprivileged fear they will not gain the privileges democracy demands for them and their children. Some fear the *status quo;* others would die to preserve it, fearing the change that might follow. There is fear of individual, class, nation, and now race. Fear is not an abstraction; it is incarnate. Revolutionary man sees fear personified. The "exploiter" is a person; so, too, is the "revolutionist." He fears not the idea but the person who is the idea. It is a short journey from fear to hate. Hates are directed against persons who incarnate ideas, and it is the property of hate to seek the destruction of the object hated. Force enters the arena. Fear drives out reason. Men refuse to listen, tolerate no opposition, decline to study the idea and seek rather to destroy the person who holds the idea. Reason is ruled out at the very moment reason is most essential. Problems cannot be solved save by reason; and it is the solution of problems that is demanded by revolution. Fear can be driven out by faith. Reason and faith are compatible. If through the preaching of the eternal validities man comes to believe in brotherhood and justice, in the infinite worth of persons and the transforming power of love, in the efficacy of the service motive and the freeing power of truth; if there can be developed agreement upon objective and faith in the possibility of its realization and the intention of the people to reach it—such faith creates the atmosphere in which reason breathes. The faith that removes fear is a contribution of the first order in a revolutionary epoch. But the proclamation of the will of God must be clear and courageous, in the spirit of the prophets who did not seek to find the compromising phrase that takes enough away to include all and thereby lose all but who declared:

"Let justice roll down as waters, and righteousness as a mighty stream"; "Thus saith the Lord."

There is yet time in some lands for revolution by consent. Preaching may have a prominent part in winning the necessary consent.

III

One of the fundamental tasks is that of reconciling the necessities of brotherhood with the necessities of technology. It is not sufficiently realized that those who own the instruments and means of production also, by the very fact of ownership and control, exercise a dominant role in political life and determine in large measure the kind of life the masses live. It is the consent of ownership that is vital. If consent can be had to effect those changes necessary to introduce the democratic principle into the work life; to regard the productive machine as an instrument by which the necessary, the useful, and the beautiful may be created; to give the motive of service priority over the acquisitive motive; to guarantee full production by full employment, full use of the machine and materials—then the transition can be made peaceably, because the ordinary man who has shared the benefits of democratic freedom is willing to accept slow progress if only it is steady and its movement in the direction of abundant life for all. If fear and greed, ignorance and inertia, estop the procedures of consent, masses may adopt the procedures of coercion. To refuse reform is to choose revolution.

Men, women, and little children, for the first time in history, have come to believe that it is now possible to end hunger, banish disease, erect decent habitations—in a word, that the physical necessities can be the possession of all. Man is resolved that what ought to be must be because it can be. Hope is in his heart. The interrogations that, like the thunders of Sinai, rushed to the mind of Edwin Markham when he gazed in indignation upon The Man with the Hoe became prophetic affirmations when he looked into the eyes of the Man with a Hope:

> Tyrants, the Tools begin to think;
> And the long bondage, link by link,
> Is breaking. Out of the ancient night
> A new world rises, vast with might.
> A star breaks on the chaos—lo,
> The Shapes of the Dark begin to go!

The age-old story of the worker is told, and finally comes the clarion call:

> Behold, O World, the Toiler thinks!
> Now these old questions of the Sphinx
> Will have their answers. In this pause
> Are epochs, institutions, laws—
> The fall of Anarchy and Chance—
> The crumble of Brute Circumstance—
> The building of the Comrade State,
> To be a new benignant Fate—
> The rise of Beauty to her throne,
> To make all hearts her very own.

And, in true Markhamesque shout, the poem ends:

> Behold the Morning of the World! [5]

Is it to be the morning of battle or the dawn of brotherhood?

[5] Edwin Markham. Reprinted by permission.

In recent history revolutions have been confined largely to national boundaries; we speak of the Russian Revolution, the Chinese Revolution. But ideas, like seed borne by the wind, know no boundaries. They take root wherever there is fertile soil. The revolution of our day is a world revolution, affecting all peoples, all nations, all classes, all religions. Its bewildering manifestations are seen in a few unrelated questions. What of the morrow in European economics? The industrial life of Europe was built up in national spheres, but no nation was a valid economic unit. Hence, as German power was extended, the heretofore national economies were brought into an economy that became continental in scope. Will Europe return to competing national economies? If not, will the continental economy be operated on fascist or communist lines? Who will control it? What changes in social custom are likely to follow the practices of a war in which rich and poor alike were mobilized to serve in the industries of the nation when its life was at stake? What will come after the common use of air-raid shelters, after the rationing of foods that all might have enough or at least a just share and that no matter what one's wealth he could not surfeit himself while others were hungry? What will be the response of owners of natural resources when the people demand that we must move from liberty to equality if fraternity is to be achieved? Is there danger that this war, fought with such utter courage and incredible sacrifice, may be but the prelude to fratricidal strife and that the war of the nations may become a war of the classes?

David E. Lilienthal, Chairman of the Tennessee Valley Authority, has written an extraordinary book entitled *TVA*

–*Democracy on the March.* It is his belief that "people are hungry these days for some specific way in which they can translate their religious feeling into concrete and realizable form."

"The book is, in reality, one with a moral and religious theme. It insists that economic development must have an ethical purpose and adopt means that further human dignity and social responsibility." He writes:

> Here men and science and organizing skills applied to the resources of waters, land, forests, and minerals have yielded great benefits for the people. And it is just such fruits of technology and resources that people all over the world will, more and more, demand for themselves. That people believe these things can be theirs—this it is that constitutes the real revolution of our time, the dominant political fact of the generation that lies ahead. No longer do men look upon poverty as inevitable, nor think that drudgery, disease, filth, famine, floods, and physical exhaustion are visitations of the devil or punishment by a deity.
>
> Here is the central fact with which statesmanship tomorrow must contend. The political promises that will be made and the great popular movements that will rise will deal with the demands of people for the ever larger harvest that science and nature, devoted to a common purpose, can be made to yield. The terms under which the people of the world will receive the products of technical advance, such as those that have come to this valley in the decade past, are at the vortex of the cyclonic forces of our century.
>
> This hour, moreover, is the right time for telling of such things. In the desperation of a fight to survive, miracles have been wrought in laboratories and with machines. Seeing the reality of things they had never dreamed could happen, men have been deeply stirred; now almost nothing seems impossible. Whether on the fighting fronts or tending the home sector,

men are thinking of tomorrow, thinking of it with longing tinged with fear and uncertainty, livened with hopes for the future. Those who fight and others who produce that their brothers may be able to fight want an earnest of good faith as to that future—things that they can see, can themselves experience. They seem no longer greatly moved and lifted by abstractions. Their thinking is less complicated but closer to life than that of the intellectual on the lecture platform or the political leader drafting a manifesto.

The fight itself comes first. But beyond that there are pictures in the recesses of men's thought behind the fighting: sixty acres of land, how it can be brought back to fertility; how to dehydrate or freeze the crop for the best kind of market; how to get back on a job at a new kind of factory machine at good pay; about a pleasant town where the kids can have bicycles; about electric lights and heated schools and churches and hospitals for the ill; no more flooding out every spring; long Diesel barges on the river to carry off the warehoused wheat; refrigerators and irrigation canals and an end to the malaria mosquitoes. The word spreads that these and many other things can be realized after the war, that the inventors and engineers and chemists can make them happen. The word has spread to the crossroad towns in the Ozarks, the trailer camps in Detroit, the boarding houses in Fall River; to men in the oil fields across the Rio Grande, the collieries in Wales, the shops of Leeds and Manchester; even to the villages on the Ganges and the caves beneath Chungking.

Our faith is sustained by the inspiring words of great leadership, by the pledges of freedom and prosperity and democracy. But it is when the words unbend—when they come into men's homes, to their farms, their shops—that they come alive to men. . . .

But everything depends upon *how* this job is done.

The spirit in which the task is undertaken; its purpose, whether for the welfare of the many or the few. . . .

The physical achievements that science and technology now

make possible *may bring no benefits,* may indeed be evil, unless they have a moral purpose, unless they are conceived and carried out for the benefit of the people themselves.

May I conclude the quotation from Mr. Lilienthal with this striking statement:

> Faith is the greatest power in the world of men, the most "practical" force of all. How is faith sustained and built ever stronger? By the redemption of faith through works.[6]

Isaiah would repeat today: "The people that walked in darkness have seen a great light." That is indeed the most significant fact confronting contemporary leadership. In the past an occasional dreamer, prophet, or thinker saw the light. These men of light too often were destroyed by the multitudes who walked in darkness, but today the people have seen a great light. Like a person who stands in the darkness of a desert just before the dawn, they have looked toward the ranges and have seen the first faint line of carmine that defines the mountain tops; and in that light they have read a promise, the promise of a new day. The masses, for good or ill, have come to believe that abundant life is possible. They are resolved to possess it. The educator, scientist, poet, and preacher have kindled a fire in the mind of man, the fire of faith, a fire that cannot be extinguished. It is prophecy and portent.

IV

With this belief in their hearts, the masses ponder the proposals that come from revolutionary as well as reform

[6] New York: Harper & Bros., 1944, pp. 3-6, 222.

movements. The preacher would do well to note that the major revolutions of our day have been accompanied by a repudiation either of Christianity itself or of Christianity in its organized form, the Church. It is not the salvation promised by other religions that constitutes the challenge to Christianity's place in the minds of men. It is rather the promise of equality and fraternity proclaimed by communism and other social and economic philosophies. It is a strange shortsightedness that trains the future minister in comparative religion—and properly so—but fails to equip him to face the dynamic competitors who preach a new faith and hold out the promise of a new world. The preacher must know the fundamental causes of the revolutionary era into which he has been thrust, must know the ideals proclaimed by revolutionary movements, the programs proposed and the methods advocated to realize these ideals. He must come to decision relative to the great objectives for man and society—thus being in a position to continue as the teacher of the principles of conduct for the individual and the group, a voice of judgment on those practices that contradict the principles, and a herald of a new day.

Once the worker was owned. Slavery was taken for granted. Although a few rebellious souls struggled against their lot, the masses turned in their rude tools at night and threw themselves down to sleep in the knowledge that the morrow would find them yet slaves. But the doom of slavery was written into the nature of things. It violated the moral law. Man is a being of worth; it is immoral to own him as property and to think of him as a tool.

With feudalism, a military system of land tenure, the worker was serf, not slave, attached to the land but possessed of certain rights and obligated to certain duties. His lot was somewhat improved, but his life was little more than that of the beast. Privileges were the possession of the aristocracy. True enough, they were supposed to recognize certain obligations that were a part of nobility; but privilege does not make for true nobility, nor does charity distributed to inferiors make for democracy. The serf began to think of liberty. A François Villon could sing: "We are good for nothing but to die; let us die for liberty."

At last the genius of man brought forth the steam-driven machine. Handicraft industry was superseded, the factory arose, vast populations crowded about the centers of work. Labor was divided and a man made a part of a shoe, a part of a wagon. He worked at a machine owned by someone else, a machine upon which he was dependent for bread. He had moved up from slave to serf, from serf to wageworker. A new freedom had come. He was no longer attached to the soil. He could move from place to place. It was *his* labor that *he* sold. But the security, such as it was in serfdom, was gone. The driving force of the new order was the search for profit. A kind of moral sanction was given to the unrestricted play of self-interest because it was held that the resulting competition in the long run worked out for social good. If one man charged too much, a competitor would reduce the price and thus force the first to meet the new price. If poor materials were produced, the purchaser would reject them for good materials. The owner set the wage, determined the conditions of work; and under the accepted morality the free worker was free to starve or take what was offered. Without doubt, during its first century the new order produced more goods than man had ever produced. Standards of living did rise. But the worker soon faced the fact that his return from labor was scarce enough to feed, house, and clothe himself and his family. He saw great fortunes rise, but he faced a level beyond which he did not rise. True enough, the new freedom gave to many the opportunity to struggle up and to become a part of the managing, the owning, class. Nevertheless, the masses lived in hunger, poverty, and dirt.

The worker realized that freedom of contract was but legal fiction unless the bargaining at contract negotiation was by bargainers approximately equal. The organization of labor followed. It was resisted by every power available to the people of privilege. Labor moved to legal status. The trade unions became a part of the social life. Along with the development of workers' organizations went the extension of the privileges of political democracy. The industrial revolution and democracy were twins. The owners of the machine controlled the state and responded grudgingly to the demands of the people expressed by the ballot. Beneath the struggles from slavery through serfdom and early capitalism lay the conflict between those who were resolved to retain their privileges and those who were determined that life should be more than toil for others.

The conflict of interest carries into the present situation. The chief beneficiaries of capitalism have temporized with fascism; in fact, at first, in desperation they espoused it rather than make basic adjustments in the interest of equality—perhaps fearing that concession to democratic demand might be the prelude to communism. The Nazis moved to power in the day of appeasement because the leaders of European states preferred to acquiesce in Nazi assumption of power rather than to accommodate themselves to the changes demanded by their own peoples, which they feared might lessen their privileges. The Nazis seized the advantage and laid their plans on the assumption that the capitalists who would not fight fascism abroad would tolerate it at home. They moved by way of fifth columns during peace into the very lands they planned to attack in war. Chamberlain, who could witness the Fascist conquest of Abyssinia, Austria, and Spain and could share in the betrayal of Czechoslovakia, realized too late that the very privileges he sought to preserve for his class were themselves jeopardized by the brutal powers he had appeased.

It is hard for us to face the fact that our economic order has been one in which real power has been held by the upper and middle classes and that, true to history, the controlling groups have sought to rule the state itself and thus preserve the status of privilege. Theoretically, in democracy power rests in the people. Political power does. But there is economic power. That power lies in the ownership of the means of production, and those who sell labor for a wage are in actual fact dependent upon those who own the machines. It is true that democratic nations responded to the insistent demand of the people expressed in the vote by instituting social services. Great gains were made in education, health, public institutions of many kinds. This meant a rising standard of life. It was possible to make these grants and still maintain the system as long as the industrial nations lived in an expanding market. But with the growth of other industrial nations the competition for the world market became bitter.

The first World War saw the industrial development of the colonies and of backward peoples. The expanding market became a contracting market. The demands of the masses increased. Some called for more than social services. They demanded fundamental changes in the economic life which would remove the bases of exploitation, as they phrased it. Into this came the Russian Revolution. New ideas were abroad—and ideas are not held in quarantine at national borders by immigration officers. The new ideas challenged the fundamental assumptions of capitalism. Capital became fearful. It knew that a generation of men had been taught how to use arms and that men were conditioned to the use of force.

The youth who had been trained in the ways of violence returned to insecurity. He demanded a way to security; but his leaders were unable to point out the road, much less to lead him down it. The owners of property began to wonder if their titles to property were secure. Some held that the root cause of their insecruity lay in democracy itself, arguing that the masses with the vote could effect not only changes in terms of social services but more fundamental change in terms of social revolution. The fascist understood; offered an antidote to radicalism; and promised the protection of property, the destruction of communism, and the discipline required by an orderly society. If parliaments could become but ratifying bodies, with real decisions made by a Leader who was opposed to the dread specter of Bolshevism, perhaps property might be saved and, with it, privilege; and, of course, the Leader would be amenable to reason, or would be ruled if necessary. So the privileged owners turned to the right; and men like Fritz Thyssen financed the Leader, who was in reality no more a lover of the owners of property than of the propertyless proletariat. The Leader was out for power, loyal to no morality save that demanded to retain power, a gangster in the halls of government. Youth turned to him. He was all things to all men. To the privileged he promised protection of property. To youth he promised adventure. To the worker he promised security. Cleverly, he found the scapegoat to which he could ascribe all blame and to which he could direct all hate—the Jew, whom he condemned as the scheming beneficiary at once of Bolshevism and of capitalism. The professional class was told that denials of opportunity were due to the seizure of positions by the Jews. The capitalist was taught that communism was a Jewish creed. The worker was informed that capitalism was controlled by international bankers who were Jews. The Jew must be exterminated, said the Leader. The Leader knew what he wanted and how to get it. He wanted power; so he united the people in a sham battle, and as they fought he stole their liberty. Fascism was born.

Others saw the difficulty not in democracy but in the fact that the productive machine was privately owned, and they turned to the left under the demand for the social ownership of the means of production. Communism came.

In lands that turned neither to fascism nor to communism the great property interests turned to government for relief during depression, but they soon re-formed their forces and organized to block reform. The reforms necessary to avoid revolution were attacked with bitterness, and leaders who saw the menace that lay in fascism and who repudiated the proposals of communism failed to win co-operation in setting up reform that would insure the continuance of free enterprise. Privilege blinded the privileged to their own interests. Tension increased.

The war came. National self-preservation, plus a deep and

abiding love of country and a fuller understanding of the real menace of fascism to all free peoples, brought unity. But it is the unity of a truce, and it is not the Truce of God. It is the truce of self-interest. Business looks with fear and greed upon the vast plant built by government for war production—fearful that it means an extension of government action in the economic sphere, greedy to secure the plant for a song and thereby strengthen the hold of monopoly. Labor gives itself to war production, but eyes ownership with suspicion. It sees the scuttling of the National Resources Planning Board. It finds its own inexcusable mistakes, resulting from the action of a few of its leaders who have failed to keep the no-strike pledge, played up in the public press until the middle classes think labor unpatriotic and treasonable when, as a matter of fact, the overwhelming majority of labor have produced at full speed. The public does not know that refusal of management to act in settling real grievances that cause strikes is of a piece with strike action by labor to force settlement. Owners who refuse and workers who strike are both endangering the republic and both subject to censure. But it is particularly dangerous to develop an antilabor attitude in the minds of our soldiers and sailors, since our very future lies in the ability of management and labor to work together through the recognition of labor unions and collective bargaining. We have trained our youth for war. They have become expert in the use of weapons. It would be tragic if they were to return inflamed against labor and without knowledge of the fact that labor has given itself patriotically to full production in its pledge to win the war. The seeds of class war lie in misinforming our armed forces, and those responsible for sowing them do the nation a terrible disservice. Owners who see in this situation an opportunity to deliver a telling blow against labor are blind to their own interests.

The conflict is in temporary suspense. Are we to move into bitter struggle at home the moment we have ended struggle abroad?

V

Is the preacher to be but a voice crying in the wilderness? He may properly summon men to repentance; but "Repent ye" must always be prelude to the greater announcement, "The kingdom of heaven is at hand." Men may kneel in repentance, but they must stand upon their feet to march. It is marching that is needed; and the command must be now as then, "Follow me." People will not follow unless they hold that Christ's way, truth, and life lead to brotherhood and justice. Such brotherhood must live in all the relationships of men. Such justice must be the foundation upon which the structure of practice is reared. The people are done with slogans. Stones will not suffice for bread. The preacher who is to be heard must make it abundantly clear that his gospel is relevant to the problems of the age.

Is there a sadder fact in contemporary society than that of a people whose engineering genius has made them so efficient that plenty is possible but whose ethical blindness and organizational incapacity doom them to scarcity? Efficiency is of little avail if men are not clear as to the ends they would attain by the application of their efficiency. Our very genius, Nemesislike, pursues us. We can produce but cannot distribute in a moral or rationally adequate way. Is it because of inherent fallacies in the system itself? It does become the concern of religion when the factors of production, distribution, and consumption work against each other. It is the high privilege of the preacher to give man such a sense of ends, such a unifying purpose, that our genius may be freely expended and man thereby become free indeed. The powers inherent in democracy must be released. The war has revealed what can be done by free peoples when there is common objective. He must make it clear that a people who have waged war to preserve the privileges of all the people do not intend to move into a peace that re-establishes the privileges of the few.

These adjustments should be made by consent. It is a function of the Church to create the spirit upon which change by consent depends.

The preacher is pledged to the necessities of brotherhood. The work life of man is determined by the necessities of technology. Can the necessities of brotherhood and the necessities of technology be reconciled? To bemoan mass production and to call for a return to the handicraft methods of medievalism is to make ourselves ridiculous. The assembly line is here to stay. But can the assembly line become an instrument of brotherhood as well as of production? Not as long as the worker is regarded either as commodity or as tool! When the assembly line is an instrument to produce for man and the worker knows that the labor he expends is returned in better living, when the democratic principle is carried to the work life and the worker shares in determining the conditions under which he works and also makes his creative contribution to work, when the primary end is personality rather than profit, then work takes on spiritual significance as making possible fullness of life for all men, the process becomes an act of brotherhood, and the product the possession of brothers. It is not toil that breaks the spirit of the worker; it is toil for those who appropriate the surplus, and thereby live upon the worker, that destroys his spirit.

Thoughtful men know that it is not less work but more that man craves. The universal obligation to work must be written into the codes of the morrow, and he who will not work may not eat. But the fruits of labor must go to labor; and labor must be conceived as work of hand and brain, essential to the conduct of the productive process. A man's standing must be determined by his service. It is the creative genius who will be most honored; and that creativity will express itself in science and art, in education and religion, in executive and organizing skills—in a score of areas. The teacher who brings the lighted mind to succeeding generations of young people, the mother who reveals in her person the love and the service upon which continuing society depends, as well as the builder of railroads and the designer of great ships of the air, will be among the honored ones. In a money-making economy we think of the important people of the community in terms of the wealth they possess, not of the service they have rendered. When the necessities of brotherhood have been enthroned at the place wealth is produced, brotherhood will be more nearly approximated in the areas where it is consumed.

New creative forces are about to be released. It becomes the preacher to distinguish clearly between the dynamic forces moving to power and the spent forces seeking to retain power. What are the barriers to the release of creative contributions? Is the primary difficulty in the fact that decision is made in terms of property rather than personality? What unseen hand keeps the machine, the material, and the man apart?

Arnold J. Toynbee, in *The Study of History,* believes the breakdown of civilization occurs when there is a

loss of creative power in the souls of the creative individuals, or the creative minorities, who have been the leaders of any given civilization at any given stage in this history of its growth. . . . This failure of vitality on the leaders' side divests them of their magic power to influence and attract the uncreative masses. Where there is no creation, there is no mimesis. The piper who has lost his cunning can no longer conjure the feet of the multitude into a dance; and if, in rage and panic, he now attempts to turn himself into drill-sergeant or a slave-driver and to coerce by physical force a people whom he feels that he can no longer lead by his old magnetic charm, then, all the more surely and more swiftly, he defeats his own intentions; for the followers who have merely flagged and fallen behind as the heavenly music died away will be stung by the touch of the whip into active rebellion.

We have seen, in fact, that when, in the history of any society, a Creative Minority degenerates into a mere Dominant Minority which attempts to retain by force a position which it has ceased to merit, this fatal change in the character of the ruling element provokes, on the other side, the secession of a Proletariat which no longer spontaneously admires, or freely imitates, the ruling element, and which revolts against being reduced to the status of an unwilling "under-dog"! We have also seen that this Proletariat, when it asserts itself, is divided from the outset into two distinct parts. There is an "Internal Proletariat," prostrate yet recalcitrant, under the Dominant Minority's heel within the disintegrating society's borders, and an "External Proletariat" of barbarians beyond the pale who now violently resist incorporation. And thus the breakdown of the civilization gives rise to a class-war within the body social of a society which was neither divided against itself by hard-and-fast divisions nor sundered from its neighbors by unbridgeable gulfs so long as it was in growth.

On this showing, the nature of the breakdowns of civilization can be summed up in three points: A failure of creative power in the minority, an answering withdrawal of mimesis on the part of the majority, and a consequent loss of social unity in the society as a whole.

Revolutions are violent because they are the belated triumph of powerful social forces over tenacious old institutions which have been temporarily thwarting and cramping these new expressions of life. The longer the obstruction holds out, the greater becomes the pressure of the force whose outlet is being obstructed; and the greater this pressure, the more violent the explosion in which the imprisoned force ultimately breaks through.

It will be seen that, whenever some new aptitude or emotion or idea arises in the life of any society, this new force is likely, in proportion to its strength and its range and its importance, to come into collision with a greater or lesser number of the society's existing institutions, and each of these collisions may have any one of three alternative outcomes. The obstructive institution may either be brought into harmony with the new force promptly and peaceably through some constructive social adjustment; or it may be eliminated tardily and violently through a revolution; or it may succeeed in defying both adjustment and elimination, and in this last event some social enormity will result from the unnatural "drive" which will now be put into the intractable institution automatically by the new force that has failed to master it. It is evident that, whenever the existing institutional structure of society is challenged by the impact of a new social force, each and all of these three possible alternative outcomes of the collision may actually be realized simultaneously in respect to the different parts of the structure; and it is further evident that the ratio in which the three outcomes are represented in the total result of this particular round of Challenge-and-Response will be a matter of momentous importance in the working out of the society's destiny. Retardation is . . . of the essence of revolutions; and it is this that accounts for the violence which is their most prominent feature.[7]

VI

It is the preacher's task to create the spirit that will make it possible for new creative forces, which are persons, to meet with elements of retardation, which are persons, and in that spirit to bring the play of reason to bear upon the essence of our faith, to the end that the creative forces now spent and the creative forces yet dynamic may unite to achieve realizable goals that brotherhood demands rather than engage in fratricidal strife in which energies that might have been given to construction are wasted in destruction. In such a task the parties involved think of measures. The preacher has proclaimed ideals. He must be careful lest he identify the absolutes of his faith with the measures of proposed solution. We move to the absolute by way of the relative; but the absolute must be held before us, forever beckoning and inspiring. When the preacher identifies Christianity with the co-operative, the trade union, socialism, communism, capitalism, he has made the transitory the eternal in the thought of followers; and when the so-called eternal passes, his authority passes too. However, there is less danger of making this mistake than of attempting nothing under the counsel of caution.

The chiropractor is said to be versed in spinal adjustment. Some people, I am told, have become healthy after the treatment. I cannot speak from experience, but descriptions of treatment have left me a bit awed and very doubtful.

[7] London: Oxford University Press, 1939, IV, pp. 5-6, 135-36.

Nonetheless, I think we need chiropractors. There are too many of us like Mr. Burbank's cactus—spineless. Whether the chiropractor can put a new spine in the spineless, I do not know; but I am for anyone who can put a strut up the backbone of Christians suffering from curvature.

Perhaps the preacher will do well to be closer to the persons who are leaders in the vast movements of change—better yet, more intimately acquainted with the conditions that create the demand for change. I have talked much about unemployment, but I have never been out of work. I have never returned to my home forced to confess to my wife and children that no one wants my hands or brain. I have taken collections for famine relief, but I have never been hungry. How can I speak for that majority of mankind who lie down to sleep in hunger? My grace before meals has been, "We thank thee for these blessings." Millions of my brothers pray, "Give me this day my daily bread." When my children have been ill I have called physicians and surgeons and have consulted specialists. How can I know the heart of a father who looks upon the closed eyes of a daughter who might have lived had he been able to provide similar care?

Years ago my brother played on the All Southern California football team. In those days there was no soft turf. One had to be a man to play football. The winner of the game between Stanford and California played for the championship of the state against All Southern California. Stanford won and came south for the game. During the first half Stanford gained considerable ground. My brother played center. The man who played guard on his right was named Morgan. "Monk" they called him. He was a giant—weighed two hundred fifty pounds and was so big that when he got down in the line he looked like an ordinary man standing up. But he was the type of person who did not move too rapidly unless occasion demanded. There was fight in him, but football was a game. Between halves the coach came to my brother and said, "Ox, what's the matter with Monk?" My brother answered, "Nothing that I know of." The coach was of the rough type of days gone by and broke in, "I didn't ask you to say 'Nothing's the matter'; I asked you 'What's the matter?' " So my brother hazarded a guess: "I think, Coach, maybe Monk isn't mad yet." The coach flashed an understanding wink and whispered, "Can you pass the ball with one hand?" My brother thought he could. "All right, then, you do just what I tell you." I do not discuss nor condone the ethics of the order. "When you go back in there, I want you to get your right hand full of dirt. Pass the ball with your left, swing your right hand and rub that dirt in Monk Morgan's eyes. When he gets up, you tell him that Stanford guard did it." The orders were carried out, and for good measure my brother swung his hand back with considerable force. When Monk got down for the next play, he twisted his head around and growled, "Say, Ox, who hit me?" My brother pointed to the Stanford guard, and said, "He's making a fool out of you." When the ball was snapped from then on, there was a hole in that side of the line large enough for a freight train to go through.

Men sometimes learn to see when the dirt of the world is in their eyes!

There is a sinful heart beneath revolution, and a sinful society too. Both must be born again. Whosoever believeth on Christ may find new life. It is the high duty of the preacher to make man see that revolution and reform are not enough;

regeneration is demanded. It is an age in which revolution may be had by consent in some areas; in others the hour is late and violence comes with the morning. Whether the sorry scheme of things is molded a little nearer the heart's desire will depend not alone upon the measures of the changers but upon the spirit of the changeless, not alone upon discovery of economic law but upon obedience to the moral law, not alone upon the rule of man but upon the Son of Man regnant among the redeemed.

CHAPTER II

A COMMON FAITH AND A COMMON PURPOSE

Konrad Heiden, in his study of Hitler's rise to power entitled *Der Fuehrer,* concludes:

> Hitler was able to enslave his own people because he seemed to give them something that even the traditional religions could no longer provide; the belief in a meaning to existence beyond the narrowest self-interest. The real degradation began when people realized that they were in league with the Devil, but felt that even the Devil was preferable to the emptiness of an existence which lacked a larger significance.
>
> The problem today is to give that larger significance and dignity to a life that has been dwarfed by the world of material things. Until that problem is solved, the annihilation of Naziism will be no more than the removal of one symptom of the world's unrest.[1]

Harold J. Laski, in the closing lines of his analysis of communism, writes:

> Communism has made its way by its idealism and not by its realism, by its spiritual promise, not its materialistic prospect. It is a creed in which there is intellectual error, moral blindness, social perversity. Religions make their way despite these things. Mankind in history has been amazingly responsive to any creed which builds its temple upon spiritual heights. The answer to the

[1] Boston: Houghton Mifflin Co., 1944, pp. 773-74.

new faith is not the persecution of those who worship in its sanctuary, but the proof that those who do not share its convictions can scan an horizon not less splendid in the prospect it envisions nor less compelling in the allegiance it invokes.[2]

Is it true, as Heiden affirms, that the traditional religions no longer provide a "belief in a meaning to existence beyond the narrowest self-interest?" Is the prospect Christianity envisions less splendid and the allegiance it invokes less compelling than that of communism? In the ritual for the ordination of elders the bishop, after charging the candidate with the excellency and the difficulty of the office, reads: "And now, that this congregation of Christ here assembled may also understand your purpose in these things, and that this your promise may the more move you to perform your duties, you shall answer plainly to these things which we, in the name of God and his Church, shall ask of you touching the same." The minister is to preach and to practice. His faith must become purpose, and the purpose must become an act.

There are those who insist that the fascist and the communist win a hearing and maintain a following because they demand that creed be validated in conduct and that party policy be expressed in party practice. Jesus made no less a claim upon those who would be his disciples: "Follow me"; "Go, sell that which thou hast;" "Ye must be born again;" "Let your light so shine;" "Take up the cross." These are commands that assume faith, purpose, action. In the life and teaching of our Lord the act expresses the purpose and the purpose reveals the faith; thus we address him, "O Thou, whose deeds and dreams were one!"

2 *Communism* (New York: Henry Holt & Co., 1927), pp. 250-51.

The gospel is preached in tens of thousands of pulpits; and the prayer of God's Son, "Thy Kingdom come," is repeated by hundreds of thousands of worshipers. Many assume that the preacher's task is done when the sermon is delivered and that the worshiper's obligation is met when he has respectfully listened. When Jesus discussed the question of inheriting eternal life, he readily agreed that men who had loved God and neighbor would inherit; but his understanding of faith was soon made clear when he dealt with the concrete question, "And who is my neighbor?" A child could understand the story of the Good Samaritan; certainly the lawyer did. But Jesus did not follow the pedagogy of the professional storyteller and allow the story to point the moral. The moral was clear. Jesus wanted both understanding and action. "Go, and do thou likewise," he said. The preacher who thinks his task is done when the benediction is pronounced and assumes enough has been said when he repeats the words of the Master, "He that hath ears to hear, let him hear," would do well to remember the command, "Go, and do thou likewise," as well as the related suggestion, "He that hath eyes to see, let him see." If his eyes see, they will look upon the tragic fact that in the major revolutions of our day the revolutionary movement has repudiated either Christianity itself or the organized expression of Christianity, the Church. Why?

I

At the very moment when millions are deaf to the preaching of religion, millions have listened to the preaching of revolution. The fascist has been heard! The communist receives a hearing!

I recall the impression made by a half-dozen German girls

of eighteen or twenty years of age when they told a group of Americans what National Socialism meant to German youth. These young women were most attractive, representative of German strength and beauty at their best. Their enthusiasm was contagious. They possessed the fire of communist youth, but it had been lighted by a contradictory ideology. They saw a new world upon the horizon, and were marching toward it. One young woman, after describing the physical education that made youth strong for service and the intellectual discipline that made them ready for leadership, said: "I am strong; I am at work; I am proud. But there is one thing more I desire. I desire to bear a child for the Fatherland." She spoke without embarrassment, but the cheeks of our chairman were flushed. He was Professor Julius Richter, who held the famous chair of missions in the University of Berlin. Trained in the morality of pre-Hitler Germany, he struggled with an explanation but could only say, "Our young people speak very frankly." What is it that elicits such utter devotion?

I watched the young women emerging from the subways of Moscow. They were strong of body, wore overalls, were covered with mud; but there was light in their eyes. I saw them at the theater and the opera. They were builders, sharing the culture of a new society, unafraid of hard labor, uninterested in soft leisure. I saw young men and women by tens of thousands march through the Red Square in a health and physical education celebration. I met young girls who had gone into Mohammedan territory to free women from the chains of custom, and release them for the service of society. This was dangerous work, but they had gone out in pride. What drives them to such service?

The call of the "classless society" and the summons of "the New Order" meet ready response. Youth answers, and offers its life. Do the claims of the Kingdom of God evoke similar response? If not, why not?

II

The ideologies of our day are more than an expression of faith; they are a proclamation of purpose. Purpose is expressed in a program through which faith becomes practice. The communist really believes the classless society can be built, and the fascist is determined to establish the New Order. Unfortunately, when the Kingdom of God is preached, it is accompanied by certain faith-destroying postulates, such as: The Kingdom is not to be realized in history; The Religion of Jesus is an expression of perfectionist ethics; We must avoid the fallacy and recognize the futility that lie in the proclamation of the distant ideal. Christianity has been preached as faith, but Christians have too seldom insisted that there must be a Christian purpose as well as a Christian faith and that the purpose must be accompanied by the techniques by which it can be realized. Brotherhood must be expressed in institution and social practice if the philosophy of the second mile, the cup of cold water, and the crown of thorns is to hold the loyalty of youth.

A revolutionary age is an age of action. The Nazi did more than preach the doctrine of National Socialism. He moved with the "terrible single-mindedness of the fanatic" to establish the New Order. The communist has sought to understand the nature of the social process and has summoned men to the task of abolishing the exploitation of man by man. But he has not rested in study and summons; his research has been indissolubly bound to resolution. Faith and purpose are one, and he moves to establish the classless society. The Nazi appealed to a race and a nation. He spoke of blood and soil. The communist appealed first to a class. He spoke of hammer and sickle. Now he appeals to class and nation, and sings of Mother Russia. From the beginning Christianity has appealed to all mankind. It has sought to unite all men as brothers rather than to unite Nordics as a predestined elite to rule inferior breeds, or to unite the workers that they might lose their chains and, through dictatorship, set up a society that some day would be classless and in which the state itself would wither away. Is the Christian naïve when he calls for a common faith instead of a class faith, a race faith, a nation faith? No, the naïveté does not lie in the call for a common faith. It lurks in the assumption that man will respond to a faith that is not bound to a purpose. Preaching must unite men in an agreement as to ends. The ends must be realizable, and of such utter worth to man that life itself is not thought too dear to give for their realization. Preaching must declare the faith, proclaim the purpose, and enlist the individual.

The faith of our fathers was subjected to dungeon, fire, and sword. Their sons must needs have cushions in the pews. But their sons' sons, who have established beachheads under enemy fire, who have parachuted to earth and seized the power plants of the foe, who have struggled through minefields and fought hand to hand with their adversaries, are not likely to respond to the preaching of a faith that does not demand works. Unforgiveable weakness lies in a proclamation of an ideal without a corresponding charge to be partisan enough to take the action the ideal demands. A false separation of church and state has paralyzed the moral forces of the nation, who move neither hand nor foot lest religion become politics; and all the while the immoral forces in full strength seize the institutions of the state and of the economic order, determining their character in full confidence that no danger threatens them from the preachers, whose sermons never become crusade. That there is danger, grave danger, when religious man seeks to act as political man, cannot be gainsaid. But the distinction between religious man, so called, and political man, so called, will not stand scrutiny. Man is man; he is worker, citizen, churchman, father, brother, son. He has a duty as churchman to see that the faith he declares in the sanctuary becomes the practice he demands as citizen in the assembly, that the petitions of his prayers become the directives of his enterprise.

The voice of the preacher is too often the voice of protest. It is positive proposal that is needed more than negative prohibition. The religious forces of the nation must become influential at the place decision is made before it is made. Their convictions must be presented as creative and cooperative contributions. Protests may estop wrong action; proposals are necessary to inaugurate right action. Negatives are easy to discover; and this is not to object to those corrective and coercive actions that are required to keep a community clean and healthy but to point out the higher necessity of organizing the group life itself upon those positives consonant with the moral law, or, as the preacher prefers to put it, the will of God, and of discovering and applying measures expressive of that law and will. It is here that real opposition arises, and in the opposition the real faith of the opponent stands forth. Most churchmen see the menace that lurks in narcotics. They do not see so clearly the habit-forming and soul-destroying results that follow addiction to the selfishness that is accepted as essential to competitive enterprise.

Men become alert when their real beliefs are attacked. When fascism arose, there were many who believed we could accommodate ourselves to it. Appeasement was more than political policy; it was economic protection; for in fascism some saw the defense against communism that would protect their real interest, property. It was only when fascism tore off its brown shirt and revealed its naked intent that the propertied saw the danger. Mussolini declared, "Let's have done with this talk of brotherhood;" and Hitler talked about "the nothingness of the individual;" but appeasement went on. When it became clear that the fascist, like the gangster-racketeer, meant to control and to exploit what he controlled, then the men who were unalarmed by repudiations of brotherhood and denials of the worth of man became exercised. Men do act upon their faith. Lewis Mumford is right: "One cannot counter the religious faith of fascism unless one possesses a faith equally strong, equally capable of fostering devotion and loyalty, and commanding sacrifice." [3]

III

The need of common faith and common purpose is widely recognized. The distinguished members of The Commission to Study the Organization of Peace declare: "The organization of peace must have back of it the force of a unifying ideal. The sovereignty of the nation-state is no longer adequate. The alternatives are world empire,

[3] *Faith for Living* (New York: Harcourt Brace & Co., 1940), pp. 46-47.

achieved by conquest, or some form of association, such as world federation achieved by consent." They move at once from expression of ideal to search for means to realize the ideal, stating: "Unless the peoples of the United Nations comprehend the minimum requirements of a world organization able to maintain a just and lasting peace under the present conditions of technology and democracy and are prepared to accept the changes in the traditional prerogatives of national states which such an organization requires, statesmen will lack the material for sound agreement." Similarly, in the economic field the same need is found.

One of the most penetrating of contemporary political economists writes:

> We confront, in a word, the need, not for a law here, or a law there, but for a vital change in the whole spirit of government. . . . All over Western Europe and America that inner spirit of government refuses adaptation to the demands of a new time. It has broken down, exactly as the rule of the feudal aristocracy broke down, because, within the terms of its principles, it cannot exploit the potentialities of production. . . . The power to distribute fails everywhere in our civilization to keep pace with the power to produce that is at our disposal; and business men are compelled to ask the aid of the state in restricting, in the interest of their profits, the supplies which men so badly need.[4]

This brilliant writer adds: "The contradiction between the political sovereignty of numbers and the economic sovereignty of the privileged threatens the foundations of law and order."

Professor William Ernest Hocking writes in similar strain

[4] From *Reflections on the Revolution of Our Time* by Harold J. Laski, pp. 35-36. Copyright, 1943, by Harold J. Laski. By permission of The Viking Press, Inc., New York.

when facing the political problem. "Political unity has to come from a uniting deed," he declares, and "the will to exist must take the form of the will to act; there can be no united state except an active state, united in action." [5]

The need for agreement is nowhere so critical as in the field of race. A colonel, who is a churchman and a charming person socially, said recently: "There is only one answer to this race question. We must ship the Negroes back to some black-land where they can be a part of the country; or else, as matters are developing, we shall have to shoot them." And Lillian Smith, in *Strange Fruit,* pictures the wife of a Pullman porter:

> In her ears roared a train in the night. Into her mind flashed a picture of Jack, sitting in a dim Pullman, dozing or reading under the night light, educating himself in some serious book, climbing from one idea to another idea—up, up; or answering the buzz of a wakeful passenger's bell, working for her and her child, night after monotonous night, saying his thank-you-mams, his yes-sirs, swallowing hurt pride, saving his tips for that fine life they were to live up North some day, when they had enough money.[6]

It must be apparent that in the great problem areas of life—international, economic, racial—the people grope in the darkness yearning for light, the light of faith, but even more for the leadership of purpose. Fascism and communism have been able to center the life of the people upon a single purpose: in one to rule, in the other to make man master of the machine and to insure that no man lives upon the labor of another. Rejecting as we may the pagan doctrines of the

[5] *What Man Can Make of Man* (New York: Harper & Bros., 1942), p. 106.
[6] New York: Reynal & Hitchcock, 1944, pp. 38-39.

fascist and the materialistic philosophy of the communist, repudiating the method of dictatorship upon which each has relied, the important matter is to note that the faith each holds is a faith upon which he is prepared to act, for which he is ready to die, to which he gives complete allegiance, and which he honestly expects to be realized on the earth. Is it less necessary for the citizen of a land in which political liberty is a treasured possession to be united with his fellow citizen in a common purpose to use political liberty to establish economic justice? We will not barter our freedom for the pottage of security, it is said. But without the security that lies in full employment men, if they must, may choose bread rather than ballot.

The Commission on Education for Morale, of the American Association of School Administrators, declares:

> It is essential to a modern nation that its members should be bound together by common beliefs. . . . They create the framework of a "common cause" within which private individuals and groups may develop their more detailed beliefs and their special interests without destroying the public order. . . . No organized society whatever, whether totalitarian or democratic, is possible unless its members share certain fundamental beliefs. . . . The common cause known as "democracy" may be divided into five ideals, each of which must be rooted in both the understanding and the affections; love of truth, freedom under law, fellow feeling, respect for human dignity, and personal responsibility.[7]

IV

Faith and purpose must be thought of not as separated

[7] *Morale for a Free World. America and Not America Only* (Twenty-second yearbook of the American Association of School Administrators), 1944, pp. 32-105.

but as united. When faith is real, it is of necessity purpose. The communist is quite right in testing belief not by the creed of the churchman nor the platform of the politician but by the life of the former and the practice of the latter. Jesus made it abundantly clear that in final judgment it is action, not profession, that determines. "Inasmuch as ye have done it unto one of the least of these my brethren, ye have done it unto me." Such were to enter the Father's house. "Inasmuch as ye did it not to one of the least of these, ye did it not to me." Such were rejected.

The missionary of yesterday believed that millions would be lost unless he brought the words of life to them. His faith and his purpose were one, and he went to the ends of the earth to "save the lost." When Christianity is referred to as a way of life, ecclesiastical swamps become noisy with the chirping of the critics. It is said that if we center upon the way, we may lose the life. Not so! We lose the life unless it finds the way. Jesus was the way, the truth, and the life. The young revolutionary conceives of himself as a channel through which a larger purpose flows.

Olive Schreiner spent years preparing the manuscript of her great work *Woman and Labor.* It was burned in a fire that destroyed her home. She rewrote it in a single volume. "What matters it to me," she said, "if I am not at the oar when the little boat is pulled into harbor. To know that I have pulled at the oar, that is enough for me."

The communist gives himself to a cause greater than himself. The fascist has been able to recruit youth upon similar grounds. But in each case the cause is not regarded as a proposed journey to a never-to-be-reached Utopia. They expect to enter the Promised Land. Too many Christians, and too many beneficiaries of the present economic order, are like Abraham's father, Terah—content to die in Haran. Christians who sing praises to martyrs and capitalists who extol risk while denouncing proposals to give security strangely enough refuse to push out upon the desert—preferring in inexplicable contradiction to deny risk and sustain their security, perhaps to be left in Haran while the people march to Canaan.

A common purpose must become a common plan, and the common plan must be based on common consent and infused with a common desire. But back of all, permeating all, must be a common faith.

Matthew Simpson was right when he said, "Every sermon should lead to Christ." The Christ to whom the sermon leads is a marching Christ who is to be followed as well as adored. It is not enough to kneel in sacred sanctuary while the choir sings, "We do adore thee, O Christ, and magnify thy holy name." There are temples to be cleansed, lepers to be healed, lowly ones to be exalted, gardens to be faced, and crosses to be borne.

On the Sunday evening last July before he was shot by the Nazis as a hostage in the Cherche Midi prison in Paris, the Communist Deputy Gabriel Peri wrote: "I should like my fellow countrymen to know that I am dying that France may live. I have made a last examination of conscience and am satisfied. If I had to begin over again, I would travel the same road. In a few minutes, I am going out to prepare the tomorrows that sing. Adieu and *vive la France!*" [8]

Men must believe in "tomorrows that sing." These tomor-

[8] From an article in *The New York Times Magazine* by Percy J. Philip, former *New York Times* correspondent at Paris.

rows will not come by the repetition of platitude or, for that matter, by the sincere repetition of creed. The common purpose that a common faith demands will, of necessity, be less than the full requirement of the faith. The purpose must be relevant to the society in which it is to be realized. Within that society are social groupings in which the individual lives and moves and has his being. The desires of these associations are often in conflict—the trade union and the employers' association, the taxpayers and the school administrators, the medical society and the advocates of social medicine. The purpose may seek the ideal of the faith, but the measures possible are often but a partial expression of the purpose. It is because the preacher, who publishes the faith, all too often refuses to co-operate with plans that for him are compromise but which represent the most that men are willing at that moment to accept, that the men of purpose see in the man of faith the same hypocrisy he sees in them. They conclude that he does not take his faith seriously, because he will not further it by those practical efforts that lead man a little nearer; and he thinks they repudiate his faith because the plan does not express its entirety.

The faith is adequate. The problem is the adequacy of the faithful.

V

A common purpose must be developed relative to world order. The present national states constitute a world community but an ungoverned community. Attempts to bring law and order to the world are doomed to failure unless man recognizes that just political structures cannot be built upon foundations of economic injustice. When the guns were silenced in 1918, political leaders met at Versailles. The League of Nations was established. Peace had come in the political field; at least a truce was inaugurated. But the war went on in the economic sphere, and nations that were in conflict in economics were unable to maintain peace in politics. The moral obligation to bring full economic pressure to bear upon Japan in 1931 and later upon Mussolini and Hitler was disregarded, not because it would have been ineffective, but because the economic interests of the bodies upon whom co-operation depended were often related to those of the states against which the sanctions were to be applied. We realize now, as the Educational Policies Committee has said, that

> as surely as the earth turns, force and violence shall be the law; and wars of cataclysmic destruction shall be the penalty and blood and tears shall be the inheritance of that people who neglect to learn and to teach that the earth has grown smaller, that all men on it are fundamentally alike, that no human being need now lack food or shelter, and that science has made it necessary for men to live at peace if they want to live at all.[9]

The ungoverned world will be governed! By whom? It will be governed autocratically by a dominant nation, race, or class; or it will be governed democratically by a federation of nations. It is a matter of empire or union. Those who refuse adjustment in the matter of sovereignty are blind to the fact that all sovereignty, save that of the master power, is in jeopardy unless the present sovereignties unite to establish a world order that will preserve all the self-government that

[9] *Education and the People's Peace* (a report of the Educational Policies Commission of the National Educational Association of the United States and the American Association of School Administrators), p. 23.

is possible and consistent with world good. The conception of the future organization of society as held by the fascist is repugnant to free men. It is blasphemous. Who but a madman could conceive of a world in which a "superior race" is master and in which the masters choose the better of their inferiors to become the technicians qualified to carry out orders and direct the work of the servile peoples of the earth, who in turn are to be as well cared for as cattle and regarded as the robots of the ruling race? It is to be a rule of blood and iron, of master and slave. It seems incredible that any man could have thought in such terms, but men have so thought and acted. Youth were indoctrinated; the doctrine was applied in ruthlessness unparalleled; and the dream of the elite became the nightmare of men who had been free. Hitler declared, "Man lives on war, and must perish in peace." And Spengler insists, "Life is war. Can we dismiss its meaning and still retain it?" These men know the awful destruction of war; but they believe war is inevitable, necessary, and beneficent. They hold that struggle is written into the nature of things; that nature is "red in tooth and claw;" and that it is only in this struggle that the strong, who are fit to rule, emerge. Thus war is necessary to the process of natural selection, and is therefore good. They do not expect the rule of the masters to be one of peace. The masters will come to power by war and maintain their position as masters by war.

The Christian rejects these doctrines and can find no word save "devilish" to describe them. He holds that there is moral law, that there is evidence to support the belief that co-operation rather than conflict makes for progress, that it is not the predatory brute who shall survive but the creative servant; and he desires an order in which leadership is exercised by men and women who see in all human beings persons of worth and who bring truth, goodness, and beauty to mankind, thereby becoming great as they serve. Alfred Rosenberg, the Nazi philosopher, thinks of peace in different terms: "A new peace shall make Germany mistress of the globe, a peace not hanging on the palm fronds of pacifist womenfolk, but established by the victorious sword of a master race that takes over the world in the service of a higher civilization."

Are we not ready for common purpose in this suffering world, a purpose that is expressive of the mind and heart of the Saviour of the World, whose world mind, world heart, and world will summoned men long since to service in a world parish, teaching the nations, sustained by the knowledge, "Lo, I am with you alway"?

The nation is the largest unifying concept man has applied: and nationalism has been of great worth in this regard, but its work has been accomplished. Its benefits will be kept and treasured. Man now needs a larger unifying concept—one capable of uniting the classes, the races, the nations. The unity desired is both an idea and an expression of idea in organization. The world is one. There is one human family. God is the Father of all. We are of one blood. This is the idea, phrase it as we may; but the idea must have a body. The family exists.

The preacher must make men see, must summon them to act. The faith of the centuries is one—one Father, one Saviour, one family, one world. But the faith must become the act. The great commission begins with the words "Go ye."

VI

It is one thing to build a house. It is another to rear a happy family. When the architect, the contractor, and the craftsmen complete their tasks and the house is accepted by the owner, the minister may be called upon to read the ritual prepared for the dedication of a home. Its first words are, "Peace be to this house." The house is built. But the hour never comes when the father and mother can sit by the fireside and in quiet satisfaction say, "The family is reared." The happy home, the peaceful home, is one in which the members of the family have learned to live together. Each new day brings new problems, calls for new solutions, new sacrifices, new services.

The structure for a peaceful world, like a house for a family, is important; but peace must not be thought of in terms of structure alone. The plans may be agreed upon at a peace conference. The house may be built. But the fundamental task before us is that of rearing the family of God in a world house that will become a home for humanity and will last forever and forever.

If we are to think constructively about the coming peace, three words must be kept in mind. These words are "continuous," "consent," and "character." Differences arise constantly, and institutions established to settle differences must be in constant operation. It is not enough to have representatives of the nations meet once in a decade and draw up conventions that they pledge themselves to observe. Just as international action to banish disease and to preserve health calls for international health agencies continuously at work, fighting plague here, struggling against typhus there, and all the while pursuing measures in research and preventive medicine, so, too, international action must be constant in dealing with such questions as stable currency, access to raw materials, transportation and communication, and labor standards. Subject peoples come of age and declare, "Good government is no substitute for self-government." No one knows the hour when decision must be made. Upon the solution of problems, peace depends. And solution calls for agencies continuously at work. Peace is a continuous process.

Consent is equally important. Coercion will not do, except as the community enforces law established to promote the general welfare. The day of the tyrant has passed in the thinking of democratic man. Government must rest upon the consent of the governed and draw its just power from that consent. If peace is to be maintained, law must be established; and the law must express the consent of the people. No nation, or group of nations, can long dominate the world. If international anarchy is to give way before world law and order, a universal association of nations must be established. And the decisions of the universal association must be based on consent.

All of this assumes that the nations really belong to a larger entity, namely, the world community. Just as the nation has to be organized, so the world must be organized. Just as law must govern in the nation, so it must govern the world. Law does not govern in a nation unless the citizens work together for the common good, respect the law and obey it. It will not govern in the world unless there be continuous co-operation in which the factor of consent is basic.

The nation must recognize that, just as the individual is subject to the law of the nation in which he lives, the nation must be subject to the law of the world of which it is a part.

If a citizen refuses to obey the law of a democratic community, the community enforces that law in the interest of the common good. There can be no orderly community based upon anarchy. Nor can there be an orderly world based upon the principle that each nation may do what it pleases.

The nations of the world are responsible for world law; and when one nation refuses to obey that law, such disobedience becomes the concern of the world association. If the lawbreaker, whether an individual or a nation, uses force, then the community, whether nation or world association, must restrain the lawbreaker and use force if necessary. Thus the F.B.I. ended kidnapping. Thus the world association will end nation stealing.

Our individual rights are guaranteed in an orderly community. Our national rights will be guaranteed in the world community. As an individual, I am subject to the law of my community; and if I disregard my duties and disobey the law, the community restrains me. This means that every law-abiding citizen is protected and is secure. Similarly, the world community cannot allow the individual nation to be the sole judge of its own acts. Its rights are guaranteed by the world community, and it is subject to the law of that community. Thus every law-abiding nation is protected and secure.

"Continuous" and "consent" are important words. "Character" is more important. Character is fundamental to co-operation. If a man calls in a neighbor's home, ostensibly to be friendly but actually to learn the arrangement of the house so that he can break in and steal, the community becomes a place of suspicion and of hate. In fact, it ceases to be a community. The character of the citizen will determine the character of the community. Character is a matter of conviction. Thus, the most important single question related to the coming peace is this: What is your faith?

Is this our Father's world? Is moral law written into the nature of things? What is your faith? Was Mussolini right when he declared, "Since prehistoric times one shout has come down on the waves of the centuries and the series of generations: 'Woe to the weak' "? Is that the message of the centuries? Was Jesus mistaken and his sacrifice upon the cross but a sorry gesture? Must we accept the law of the jungle as the law of life; admit that nature is "red in tooth and claw;" and, as a part of this cruel order, abandon the practice of love, the hope of liberty, and the dream of abundant life for all? What is your faith? Is greatness to be found in service? Is it "Give," not "Take," that is written into the very structure of the universe?

What is your faith? Christianity affirms the infinite worth of man. Personality is the supreme good. In its declaration of the dignity of humanity Christianity proclaims the fundamental concept upon which democracy is based. In Christian faith, man is of worth because he is a son of God. We are children of one Father. We are brothers. Ultimate loyalty is not to class, race, or nation. It is to God.

Hitler has declared: "To the Christian doctrine of the infinite significance of the individual human soul and of personal responsibility, I oppose with icy clarity the saving doctrine of the nothingness and insignificance of the individual human being and of his continued existence in the visible immortality of the nation." Is that it, "the nothingness of the individual"? Or is it, "I am a son of God"?

What is your faith? Does truth free, love transform, service ennoble, and faith elevate? Have we seen the heart of the Eternal in the soul of Jesus Christ? Our Lord is indeed the unifying force in terms of perfection, God manifest in the flesh. He is the Ideal incarnate; and complete surrender to him does so affect the mind, heart, and will as to produce the character essential to this high hour. One is our Leader, even the Christ. Is that your faith?

VII

A common purpose is also demanded in the work life of man. Tools must be regarded as instruments to be used by man for man. When the tool becomes an industrial order, that tool must be similarly regarded. It is to blaspheme to think of man as a tool. Offering our sons to Moloch is a practice revolting to modern man. And someday the sacrifice of millions upon the terrible altars of Mars will be seen as the act of blind and brutal barbarians whose faith was belied by their irreverence. It may be longer before we behold Mammon in his true light. He is a greedy god. We have offered our families to this god whom Jesus refused to serve. The ancient Aztec cut the heart out of his victims. But Mammon tears the heart from the work life of mankind. His votaries are legion. They rise from our altars to kneel before his. They sing:

> All hail the power of Jesus' name!
> Let angels prostrate fall;
> Bring forth the royal diadem,
> And crown him Lord of all.

They continue: "O Love that wilt not let me go;" "O Cross that liftest up my head"; and, finally,

Were the whole realm of nature mine,
  That were an offering far too small
Love so amazing, so divine,
  Demands my soul, my life, my all.

With the words, "The grace of the Lord Jesus Christ, and the love of God," ringing in their ears, they depart from the sanctuary, with its benediction, to their rest of the night. But on the morrow they bow anew before Mammon, repeating his creed:

Self-interest is the only sufficient motive to drive men to real achievement. Moral right must bow to economic necessity. The unrestricted play of self-interest makes for social well-being. Enlightened self-interest is but the commonsense expression of Christian faith. Mammon loveth a cheerful taker. He who would be greatest among you must become the exploiter of all.

But, thank God, there is something in man, greedy though he be, that speaks out against the rule of Mammon. Man does know right and wrong, and he does know that the way of greed is not the way to eternal life. He knows his best service springs from motives other than self-interest. He gives himself for his child, for his loved ones, and thereby finds himself. A teacher realizes herself in the gift of learning and personality, never becoming the poorer. It was fitting that the millions to whom Madame Curie had been but a name associated with a strange substance called radium, to whom the story of her life exquisitely told by her daughter had been a closed book, should have beheld her in that moving moment of honor as revealed by Greer Garson in the picture *Madame Curie.* It was the twenty-fifth anniversary of the discovery of radium. The learned of the world had assembled to do her honor. The struggle of the years, the loneliness that was her lot, the generosity and the spirit of the scientist that had refused to patent and to profit, the flame that burned in the soul of this woman of genius, were all revealed as she spoke in the humility that was greatness, not the strident voice of the selfish who would master men but the friendly voice of the servant who would minister to all.

> Even now, after twenty-five years of intensive research, we feel there is a great deal still to be done. We have made many discoveries. Pierre Curie, in the suggestions we have found in his notes and in thoughts he expressed to me, has helped to guide us to them.
>
> But no one of us can do much; yet each of us, perhaps, can catch some gleam of knowledge which, modest and insufficient of itself, may add to man's dream of truth. It is by these small candles in our darkness that we see before us, little by little, the dim outlines of the great plan that shapes the universe. And I am among those who think that for this reason science has great beauty, and, with its great spiritual strength will in time cleanse this world of its evils, its ignorance, its poverty, diseases, wars, and heartaches.

Look for the clear light of Truth;
Look for unknown new roads. . . .
Even when man's sight is keener far than now,
Divine wonder will never fail him . . . .
Every age has its own dreams,
Leave, then, the dreams of yesterday;
You—take the torch of knowledge,
Perform a new work among the labors of the centuries
And build the palace of the future.[10]

[10] Reproduced by courtesy of Metro-Goldwyn-Mayer. The poem is from *Madame Curie,* by Eve Curie, copyright 1937 by Doubleday, Doran & Co., Inc.

Such is the spirit of the Christian faith!

Can belief in a Father of all, whose moral purpose is omnipresent; in the infinite worth of man, whose good must be placed before the tools he has created; in service, which enables man to express personality in creative dedication revelatory of brotherhood—can such faith be matched by a purpose so amazing and so divine as to demand our all, a purpose to create an ordered world in which the family of God may be reared in love, a purpose to make the products of human genius the servant of man, a purpose to subordinate the acquisitive drives to the regnancy of the yearning to serve and to be helpful, a purpose to use political liberty for the high end of discovering and maintaining the measures that express equality—in a word, a purpose to join with our Lord and say, "I am come that they might have life, and that they might have it more abundantly?"

One of the beautiful affirmations of the Christian faith reads:

We believe in the one God, Maker and Ruler of all things, Father of all men, the source of all goodness and beauty, all truth and love.

We believe in Jesus Christ, God manifest in the flesh, our teacher, example, and redeemer, the Saviour of the world.

We believe in the Holy Spirit, God present with us for guidance, for comfort, and for strength.

We believe in the forgiveness of sins, in the life of love and prayer, and in grace equal to every need.

We believe in the Word of God contained in the Old and New Testaments as the sufficient rule both of faith and of practice.

We believe in the Church as the fellowship for worship and for service of all who are united to the living Lord.

We believe in the Kingdom of God as the divine rule in human society, and in the brotherhood of man under the fatherhood of God.

We believe in the final triumph of righteousness, and in the life everlasting. Amen.

Such a faith must rule men who would make a revolutionary age contribute to man.

Jesus of Nazareth could speak to a few men who followed him, occasionally to the multitudes. But the preacher in a revolutionary age such as ours can address the millions; he can speak as never man spake; his voice can be heard throughout the earth. Man awaits the saving word. That word, now as before, is the Word that was made flesh. Today, as then, we must hear, "Repent: for the kingdom of heaven is at hand." But today, as then, we must also hear, "Follow me."

When I was a student in Boston, I, like all other students, found my way at last to the Old North Church of Paul Revere fame. The preacher of the morning was Bishop Lawrence, the sermon itself powerful and convincing. He chose as his text Luke 21:31: "So likewise ye, when ye see these things come to pass, know ye that the kingdom of God is nigh at hand." The altar window of the Old North Church is not of stained glass. The worshiper can look through to the tenements that surround the church, which is located in the North End, the center of the Italian population of the city. While the Bishop preached, an old woman was at work on a fire-escape platform. She was bent over a tub, no doubt doing the family washing on Sunday, when free from the regular weekday job. As I thought of her, her age, the children she had no doubt borne, the tenements, the limited life, I could not but reverse the text of the Bishop and say, "So likewise ye, when ye see things come to pass, know ye that the kingdom of God is *not* nigh at hand." So impressed was I that I took the text for my first practice-preaching sermon. The Dean, as was his wont, listened and then criticized. I had mispronounced the word "squalor." Then he turned to the weightier matters of the hour: "It is not the primary purpose of preaching to bring the divisive and debatable to the pulpit. There are hungry souls that need the bread of life; they must not be given the stone of controversy. There are the sorrowful who must be comforted, the sinful who must be saved, the struggling who must be strengthened." The Dean was right, at least partially right. The minister who makes his pulpit a forum, his opinion the gospel, the changing questions of the day a substitute for the message of the changeless, will soon pay the penalty that is always exacted. But it is also true that the preacher who never tests out in concrete situations the ethical principles he proclaims will find his message so unrelated to the world in which he lives that the changes demanded by his changeless gospel are not effected and men turn to gospels whose faith is effective.

VIII

A stable society rests upon general agreement as to the ends for which men are organized. There must be within the established form provision for adaptation to a changing environment and provision also for complete revision of the form itself if necessary. When men doubt that the ends for which men are organized are valid, or that the means can ever achieve the ends, revolution is probable. Large numbers of men no longer believe that the ends demanded by Christianity or yearned for by men who would be free can be realized in terms of the principles of an economic life grounded in self-interest and pledged to competitive struggle. The preacher must realize that the call for unity will not be heard unless the unity proposed is for the purpose of establishing justice and enthroning righteousness.

Irrational inequality lies at the base of much demand for change. To acquiesce in inequality is to deny brotherhood, but brothers in the faith who unite in prayers cease to be brothers in practice when divided by privilege. Beneficiaries of the present order look upon the mass crying for justice as the forerunner of the mob bent upon destroying their privileges. Fear enters their hearts; they refuse to listen to counsel of reason, regard reform as revolution, and resist proposals designed to bring justice. They confuse the voice of reason with the shout of revolution. Too often they fail to see that to lift the unprivileged to better living is to insure better living in peace for all.

Professor Edgar Sheffield Brightman, in a delightfully popular presentation of philosophy to a group of high-school students, said: "Everybody wants something. The practical man is the man who knows how to get what he wants. The philosopher is the man who knows what man ought to want. The ideal man is the man who knows how to get what he ought to want." Can we really become one in what we want, or, better, in what we ought to want? Men of strong will are leading powerful movements in our time, movements bent on getting what their members want. The preacher has the duty of leading movements that will become increasingly powerful, movements getting what men ought to want. Such movements raise the deeper question of spirit. The spirit that is essential to the triune good of liberty, equality, and fraternity is none other than that which leaps, artesian-like, from love. Practices that issue from greed become customs to which our children become heirs, and upon which they pay heavy inheritance tax. It is still true that the sins of the fathers are visited upon the children even unto the fourth generation. It is also true that the virtues of the fathers bless the children throughout all generations.

The common faith must come to live in the practices that make for brotherhood; the co-operative spirit must supplant competitive struggle; the objective of social endeavor must shift from profit making to personality making—not that private enterprise needs to go but that the spirit that infuses it shall be altered and the objective it pursues shall be changed. Such a faith is not the ruling faith of our day, if faith be tested by works. It is hard to change faith. Men have a tendency to believe in the system from which they have benefited. They will obey law when they feel it is written to guarantee desirable ends; but when they fear law is written to bulwark privilege, they lose the respect necessary to obedience. It simply will not do to record the achievements of yesterday. Men will revere the past when its lessons and its treasures are used to enrich the present and create a greater future. They will not honor it when set up as a barrier to the morrow. No matter how many are the miles of desert crossed, the journey never ends, the Promised Land is ever beyond the horizon. Our fathers refused to make bricks without straw, and their sons refused to eat bread in the sandstorms of the desert. They were resolved to cross the Jordan.

IX

The fear that separates brothers must give way to a certainty that unites. The Christian purpose is realizable: this must be our faith. Preaching must convince men that the application of the Christian ethic will bring greater security to the minds and spirits of all men and will elicit creative contribution from the genius for the benefit of his fellows because it obeys the law that co-operation and not selfish competition is the law of progress. Such certainty is required if fear is to be cast out and the retreat from reason ended. At the very moment when critical consideration of concrete proposal is needed, reason is shackled, fear is free, and the fearful suppress opinions in the name of security. The privileged see in minor change first steps to complete change. They resist all in the name of keeping all and turn to the leader who promises to fight rather than to the leader who promises to think.

In his Romanes Lecture, delivered in the Sheldonian Theatre, June 19, 1930, Winston Churchill, speaking on *Parliamentary Government and the Economic Problem,* faces these issues with startling realism. He summarizes the doctrines of classical economics, points out new factors that old doctrines did not consider, and in his inimitable style says:

Beyond our immediate difficulty lies the root problem of modern world economics; namely, the strange discordance between consuming and producing power. Is it not astonishing that with all our knowledge and science, with the swift and easy means of communication and correspondence which exist all over the world, that the most powerful and highly organized communities should remain the sport and prey of these preverse tides and currents? Who would have thought that it should be easier to produce by toil and skill all the most necessary or desirable commodities than it is to find consumers for them? Who would have thought that cheap and abundant supplies of all the basic commodities should find the science and civilization of the world unable to utilize them? Have all our triumphs of research and organization bequeathed us only a new punishment —the Curse of Plenty? [11]

Mr Churchill goes on to pay great tribute to democracy and particularly to Parliament, but turns by sharp illustration to a fundamental weakness when economic issues are involved. The right answer must be found, and it does not come from that discussion which is often but the pooling of impressions and prejudices, nor from a compromise which represents the satisfaction of the self-interest of the largest number of constituents. What is needed, he writes, is "high, cold, technical, and dispassionate or disinterested decision." In his sly humor and biting satire he continues:

We might have a General Election in which eight million voters were taught to sing in chorus "Make the foreigner pay" and an eight million more to chant in unison, "Give the rich man's money to the poor, and so increase consuming power"; and five other millions to intone, "Your food will cost you more." We might have all this; we probably shall! But even so we may be none the wiser or the better off.

He then recommends a Sub-Parliament, an Economic Sub-Parliament, composed of men qualified to give a scientific answer to fiscal and other problems, believing that the people might follow the judgment of such a body, and Parliament therefore be required to adopt it. He adds:

Many dangers threaten representative institutions once they have confided themselves to adult suffrage. . . . The British Parliamentary system will not be overthrown by political agitation; for that is what it specially comprehends. It will pass only when it has shown itself incapable of dealing with some funda-

[11] Oxford: The Clarendon Press, 1930, p. 14.

mental and imperative economic need; and such a challenge is now open.

It is then that Mr. Churchill climaxes his argument by declaring, "You cannot cure cancer by a majority. What is wanted is a remedy."

The preacher's thought will travel on beyond Mr. Churchill's conclusion, because he knows that a surgeon or a scientist who considers cancer subordinates all to the life of the person upon whom the cancer lives as a murderous parasite. The solution that is sought in the economic field must be one that enriches persons. The correct answer to an economic question in a Nazi economy might not be the correct answer in a democracy. The question of correctness is often a question of ethics, and the measure proposed is related to the object sought. We must discover the scientific answer to an economic problem in terms of what we want, not in terms of what I want.

It is true that blind leaders cannot lead the blind. It is also true that men are blinded by fear. At the moment when brotherly foresight is needed, men grope in the darkness of greed, stumble over their possessions, and reach out their hands for the immediate. Eyes are opened by faith, and the long-range vision that sees rising standards for all takes the place of the nearsighted insistence upon low standards for many that high standards may be retained by the few. Fearful men seek to destroy the forces that make them afraid; but it is accommodation to these forces, not their annihilation, that makes for peaceful change. The very forces they fear become factors of construction when moved by the faith that reform is possible; they become agencies of destruction when convinced that change by consent will be denied.

When the preacher affirms, "I believe in God the Father Almighty . . . and in Jesus Christ his only Son our Lord," he must make that faith meaningful in terms of action. How can belief in Jesus Christ be related to the fact that workers no longer hold that the injustice they seek to remove is caused by the meanness of their employers, although there is always the human factor in worker and employer making for discord, but rather that it is a matter of a system whose organizing principles are unjust, whose fundamental elements—such as production, distribution, and consumption—are at war with each other and therefore result in inefficiency. Is there no way whereby the faith of Jesus can be related to the issue, and the question of justice and the measures necessary thereto be determined in the light of Jesus' scale of values?

If government derives its just power from the consent of the governed—and it is seen that the people possess a political power expressed in numbers that is less than the economic power of a small part of the people expressed in money—how can change be made so that all power shall rest on the consent of the goverened, economic power as well as political power? It is precisely here that the danger to democracy is most threatening. If the people seek to bring economic power under their control and to direct it to worthy social ends, there is danger that ownership, which sees the threat to power that does lie in democracy, will abandon democracy itself in order to retain the power that lies in ownership. Reformer and revolutionist alike will do well to realize that regeneration is a need equally as imperative as change, either of consent or coercion. It is a new spirit that is our greatest need. Can religion supply it?

Hugh Walpole, in *Wintersmoon,* tells of a father and son at church. The aged rector read from the Old Testament, and the boy learned of the terrible God who sent plagues upon the people and created fiery serpents to assault them. That night, when the father passed the boy's bedroom, the boy called him, put his arms around his father's neck, and, drawing him close, said, "Father, you hate Jehovah. So do I. I loathe him, dirty bully!" We have long since rejected a conception of reconciliation associated historically with an idea of a Deity that is loathsome. God, for us, cannot be thought of as an angry, awful, avenging Being who because of Adam's sin must have his Shylockian pound of flesh. No wonder the honest boy in justifiable repugnance could say, "Dirty bully." Injustice is an offense, and inequality a stench, in the nostrils of Jehovah also. Such must be denounced by preachers in a revolutionary age; and, just as our thought of God had to be moralized to represent him to moral men, so too our conception of God's world must be made moral if man is to say in honesty, "I believe in God the Father Almighty, Maker of heaven and earth."

A generation ago John Singer Sargent painted his inspired and inspiring portraits of the prophets. Literally millions of boys and girls in our church schools have seen them in color reproduction: Amos, leaning upon his shepherd's crook, rugged and calling for righteousness; Hosea, with eyes of sympathy and expression of tenderness, speaking of the love of God. They may have united with Isaiah in worship as he stands with hands uplifted and upon his face the awe and reverence of one who has seen the Lord.

Few of the children, perhaps fortunately so, know that "The Prophets" is but a single panel in a great decorative plan. The whole is the story of man's search for God, reaching the heights in the moral conceptions of the Hebrew prophets. Sargent portrays the development of religion, through the teachings of Jesus, until at last Christianity is shown as culminating in the doctrine of redemption, the dogma of the Trinity. Here we find three figures seated upon a triune throne. They are identical. Their faces are expressionless. The color is cadaverous. They are clothed in a single robe that is wound about them. Each wears a crown; each holds a scepter. How utterly inadequate, how disappointing, how repulsive—Christianity climaxing in dogma! Christian faith does not center in explanation; it lives in experience. It is faith. It is purpose. It is action.

John Dewey may be right in declaring, "There is but one sure road of access to truth—the road of patient, coöperative inquiry operating by means of observation, experiment, record and controlled reflection." He may, if he desires, see faith as "the unification of the self through allegiance to inclusive ideal ends, which imagination presents to us and to which the human will responds as worthy of controlling our desires and choices," although some of us desire recognition of the fact of revelation; but the primary matter is not how faith is established but that there be a common faith. Dewey states:

> The reality of ideal ends and values in their authority over us is an undoubted fact. . . .The aims of philanthropists, of Florence Nightingale, of Howard, of Wilberforce, of Peabody, have not been idle dreams. They have modified institutions. Aims, ideals, do not exist simply in "mind"; they exist in character,

> in personality and action. One might call the roll of artists, intellectual inquirers, parents, friends, citizens who are neighbors, to show that purposes exist in an *operative* way. . . . The aims and ideals that move us are generated through imagination. But they are not made out of imaginary stuff. . . . The new vision does not arise out of nothing, but emerges through seeing, in terms of possibilities, that is, of imagination, old things in new relations serving a new end which the new end aids in creating.[12]

A certain unity flows from the sincere search for truth as seen among the true scientists, for the reason that East and West become one in the search for truth that is to be shared by all. The laboratory of Calcutta is like the laboratory of Chicago. But, because science reaches truth, is it necessary to say that science is the sole guide? Must we abandon the guide that lies in our understanding of value? Professor William Ernest Hocking devastatingly answers those who insist that "all the great truths are valueless and all the great values untrue." He insists, "If a healing fiction will not do the required work, he must find a healing fact." He knows there must be myths, that no one can envision the future photographically. He points out that there are temporary myths that unite men on the basis of existing passions; but there are deeper myths "more of the permanent and universal aspirations of men, such as the dream of a future human fraternity." The healing fact must be one that is simple, easily understood by all. Professor Hocking defines it: "It is the truth that the world, like the human self, has its unity in a living purpose. It is the truth of the existence of God." There is indeed a purpose, a living purpose. It is, to use Professor Hocking's phrase, "a cosmic demand."

[12] *A Common Faith* (New Haven: Yale University Press, 1934), pp. 32, 33, 44, 48, 49.

"There is all the difference between having a point of certitude and having no certitude at all." [13]

Faith becomes operative and powerful when alive in persons of purpose. Faith must become militant; but it can be militant only in militant persons, in whom purpose has become passionate.

Not long before he left us, I heard Dr. S. Parkes Cadman speak of David Livingstone. An honorary degree was to be conferred upon Livingstone by one of the great Scottish universities. Said Dr. Cadman: "There is a custom in the Scottish universities that the recipient of an honary degree is fair sport for the students and must run the gantlet of their raucous remarks. The students sit in the balcony, calling out what they please. Is the candidate for honors a soapmaker, who is to become a doctor of laws? No gift to the university will silence the greeting, 'Hi, Old Soap-Maker.' Many wondered what the students would do when David Livingstone rose to receive his degree." Dr. Cadman described him. "He stood, one arm hanging at his side; his shoulder had been torn by a lion in the forests of Africa. His skin was like leather." And what did the students do? "They rose, and stood in absolute silence."

The faith of David Livingstone was revealed in a purpose that took him to Africa and kept him there. Youth responds in respect. Is mankind ready for a common faith, a faith in God the Father, expressed in unflinching purpose to create the institutions necessary to man the brother; ready for the faith that calls for an ordered world and a society in which liberty, equality, and fraternity have become the realities

[13] *What Man Can Make of Man* (New York: Harper & Bros., 1942), pp. 57, 58, 59, 61.

of the common life; ready for a work life organized upon the principle of service and dedicated to the enrichment of personality; ready for that union of faith and purpose revealed in One who was the personification of his faith and faithful to his purpose, even unto death upon the cross?

It is with faith and purpose that the preacher in a revolutionary age has to do. And what he does may determine the morrow.

CHAPTER III

THE ONE AND THE MANY IN A REVOLUTIONARY AGE

I have watched them on parade, and have seen them struggle through the infiltration courses. I have seen a guard well-nigh frozen as he stood at his post in the bitter cold at Fort Devens and the sentries on duty in the heat at Fort Benning. In the great recreational centers I have looked into the eager, questioning, uninterested, hostile, friendly faces. And I have seen men kneel at the altars in the chapels. Soldiers and sailors, thousands upon thousands—and now they march by millions. Every land hears the tread of marching men, the rumble and roar of trucks and guns. The skies are full of ships, the sea lanes crowded too; and beneath the sea youth seeks out youth. They battle to the death. There are moments when the mass ceases to be personal. It is the Army, the Air Force, the Navy, the Marines. We use the inclusive term. The one is lost in the many.

Recently I stood in the reception center of a great fort. Civilians about to become soldiers arrived. There were conferences and tests, fair and friendly, but unavoidably taking on the character of the assembly line. The individual, the citizen, who lived in a little house with his own family, was moving down the line to become a soldier, a man under orders, to live where sent, to die if death were necessary. The civilian suit of his choice was discarded and put into a bag to be sent back home. A physical examination, measurements, fitting—down the line he went, underclothes, socks, shirt, shoes, suit. The fitting was careful; a man with poorly fitting clothes loses morale. The soldiers who were at work were kind; they too had gone down the line. Then a word from an officer about the equipment and its care and, finally, together and impressively too, the oath was taken. The man had become a soldier. His training had begun. Tomorrow, embarkation; and day after tomorrow, Tarawa or Anzio.

Soldiers, masses of men, the many! The reports of their activities are received. We lost only eleven bombers! Marines were badly cut up too, but the objective was won! The men were bombed; casualties were slight! There is something terrrifying in the fact that men can think in terms of the many and forget the one. But we do it. Then suddenly all is changed. It is your son, my son. They march by, soldiers and my son.

Both of my sons are in the service. A little more than a year ago I received a letter from my younger son. He could not tell me where he was because he was ready for embarkation. I noted the name of the chaplain who had censored the letter. I knew where he was; so I telephoned, "Chaplain, I'm coming down to see you." He understood—in fact, told me later he had written his name a bit larger than usual. "Yes," he answered, "and I would suggest you come right away." We reached the gate. The passes were there and soon we sat in the chaplain's office. A moment later a knock, and an officer who was more than a soldier was there. He was my son.

I did not say "Sir," nor did I call him "Captain." It was Phil —and my mind rushed back to the boyhood days. His mother had called him "Smiling Eyes." They were smiling then. There was mist before them now, or perhaps before my own. And so we had hours together. The Commanding Officer was kind. He gave us his car and a driver. We drove about, saw a bit of the convoy soon to sail. I sensed the tension in my son's heart. There was danger ahead and separation at hand. His wife and two little girls were far away. Then we knew that we must say good-by quickly, lest the make-believe of good spirits that all had revealed should end too soon and true feelings take control. So, "Adios, Dad. Good-by, Mother. I'll be seeing you." And when the letters came from Africa and told of the Kasserine Pass and Mateur and Bizerte, then Sicily, reached aboard a ship loaded with high-test gasoline, Salerno, and Cassino, and then the fox holes of the Anzio beachhead, I thought—and think—of one, my son.

I might speak of the other son, who wears the same uniform in pride, of his wife and his little son. But I dare not. I speak of a son, the one; and then I speak of soldiers, the many. Am I selfish? I know the many is made up of countless ones. I pray for the safety of my boy. I must pray for the safety of all. How can I bring the one and the many together in my thought?

I

This has been an age-old problem. Wise men have seen the necessity of thinking in terms of the one, of guaranteeing to the individual the fullest development of his personality; wise men have also seen the necessity of thinking of the many so that the one serves the many and the many serve the one. It has been easier for wise men to suggest these necessities than to discover the means to realize them. How can the interests of the one and the many be reconciled? In a sense, they are reconciled in war, because my son's interests and the interests of the Army are one. He desires victory, and the Army is organized to win victory. But the one and the many are not so reconciled in society, because they are not similarly united in common objective. How can we bring them together? Jesus had compassion on the multitudes. He likewise blessed Mary Magdalene.

In considering the reconciliation of the one and the many, we must see at once that the fullest development of every individual is a worthy objective. This includes the fullest development of the exceptional individual as well as the mediocre person, and thereby continues into an indefinite future the fact of inequality in talent. To restrain the exceptional in order to develop the unexceptional is to move toward mediocrity. The very development of the exceptional results in the enrichment of the human family, provided that the developed individual serves his fellows rather than exploits them. Individualism properly calls for proper consideration for the exceptional as a contribution to the community itself. But are we to think of this development as an automatic process whereby, through the "survival of the fit," the strong move to power? Are we with calm expectancy to await a so-called process of natural selection, believing that the emerging person is, of necessity, the desirable person? This is to accept tacitly the application made by Hitler of the principle found in his statement, "War is beneficent." He insists that the leadership we need is the leadership that emerges in struggle. Is that true? What becomes of the club-footed Byron; the deaf Beethoven; and the Robert Louis Stevenson, who struggles against disease? Apparently, the matter is not solved upon the basis of the survival of the physically fit. Is the determination of the exceptional to be made upon the basis of the shrewd and calculating mind, the mind that seeks for itself and destroys opposition by clever traps for the unsuspecting? What of the survival of those who have dedicated themselves to the true, the good, and the beautiful? Where do love and kindness stand? The advocates of individualism are right in demanding the freedom necessary for the fullest development of all persons and particularly of the genius. But are we to determine through education the bent of the mind, the object to which the superior mind will devote its talent? Is he to determine on his own whether he will move from paper hanger to corporal to dictator?

The individualist seldom sees that the logic of his position is that of anarchism. The anarchist—and I need not here, I trust, point out that violence is no part of the creed of the philosophical anarchist—insists that personality flourishes only when free. Thus all restraint must be removed. Limitation of freedom is limitation of personality. He calls for no government at all, no restraint of any kind. This pushes the matter, we say, to absurdity. Perhaps. But what of the doctrine that government is best which governs least? The stress upon limitation beclouds the possibilities that lie in creative service by the government to the individual. John Stuart Mill argued, as C. D. Burns puts it:

> Mankind are greater gainers by suffering each other to live as seems good to themselves than by compelling each to live as

seems good to the rest. . . . Finally and fatally, the principle that someone else knows what is good for the individual destroys the variety and originality which is the life blood of the state.

. . . .

The state should rather aim at a decentralization and dissemination of power, while a central bureau of information should de-provincialize by educating or instructing (but not governing) the local authorities . . . Power can only be shared by being decentralized; and knowledge can only be shared by being centralized.

. . . .

The worth of a state in the long run is the worth of the individuals composing it; and a state which postpones the interests of their mental expansion and elevation to a little more of administrative skill . . . a state which dwarfs its men in order that they may be more docile instruments in its hands, even for beneficial purposes—will find that with small men no great thing can really be accomplished.[1]

Classic individualism had a modern exponent in Herbert Hoover, who defines American individualism by contrasting it with other individualisms, saying:

While we build our society upon the attainment of the individual, we shall safeguard to every individual an equality of opportunity to take that position in the community to which his intelligence, character, ability and ambition entitle him; that we keep the social solution free from frozen strata of classes; that we shall stimulate effort to each individual to achievement; that through an enlarging sense of responsibility and understanding we shall assist him to this attainment; while he, in turn, must stand up to the emery wheel of competition.

He goes on to add:

[1] *Political Ideals, An Essay* (New York: Oxford University Press, 1921), pp. 242, 244, 253.

We have learned that fair division can only be obtained by certain restrictions on the strong and the dominant. . . . But for the next several generations, we dare not abandon self-interest as the motive force to leadership, lest we die.

This was in answer to the admitted growth of the ideal through education by which

selfish impulses become less dominant, and, if we ever reach the millenium, they will disappear in the aspirations and satisfactions of pure altruism.

He continues in judgment, however:

The will-of-the-wisp of all breeds of socialism is that they contemplate a motivation of human animals by altruism alone.

Mr. Hoover's acquaintance with the literature of socialism was little more than his acquaintance with social fact; for he wrote in 1922, with reference to our land,

None of us is either hungry or cold or without a place to lay his head—and we have much more besides.

However, he knows business, and writes:

It is where dominant private property is assembled in the hands of groups who control the state that the individual begins to feel capital as an oppressor. . . . Our government's greatest troubles and failures are in the economic field. . . . We found in the course of development that equality of opportunity and its corollary, individual enterprise, were being throttled by the concentration and control of industry and service, and thus in economic domination have groups builded over the nation. At this time, particularly, we were threatened with a form of autocracy of economic power. Our mass regulation of public utilities and our legislation against restraint of trade is the monument to our intent to preserve an equality of opportunity. This regulation is itself proof that we have gone a long way toward the abandonment of the "capitalism" of Adam Smith. . . . To curb the forces of business which would destroy equality of opportunity and yet to maintain the initiative and creative faculties of our people are the twin objects we must attain.[2]

He says of himself, "I am an American individualist." The very individualism he advocates has built up powerful forces destructive of the freedom of the individual. Then the many step in, he insists, and control these dominant groups once again in the interests of the free individual and of the free group. This is but another evidence of the fact that it may not be the control of the many over the one that is the real menace, but rather the control of a few individuals who gain power and thereby control not only the single individual but the individuals who, added up, mean the many.

Social legislation designed to protect workers from injustice was nullified by legal decisions based upon freedom of contract. The doctrine of individualism has been used by the strong individual to limit the freedom of the individual less strong. It was held that to establish a minimum wage was to deny the worker freedom to work for any wage he saw fit. The legal fiction ignored the exploiting fact. A man must be free to choose or reject a job, certainly; but when the job is controlled by one party to the transaction and the wages offered on a take-it-or-leave-it basis, to refuse the job is to starve. To accept it is to be party to injustice. But the worker is free to go elsewhere. On what? His wage has made savings impossible. His skill may be for a certain kind of

[2] From *American Individualism* by Herbert Hoover, pp. 6, 10, 11, 17, 33, 38, 52, 53, 54. Copyright, 1922, by Doubleday, Doran & Co., Inc.

work. He may face the same proposition in the elsewhere. There may be a labor surplus there. The question of individual liberty is not an easy one.

II

Where does liberty lie? Is a worker on a collective farm less free than a worker on his own soil? The American would answer yes; a Russian, no. There is no final yes or no.

The Russian peasant, who was really serf, became a freer man when the land passed to the people and he found opportunity to labor with his fellows, sharing in the benefit of his toil. Thus he is an individual in a collective where decisions are made by the group; but, because of present practice, he farms his own little plot apart from the collective as he sees fit, and so is an individual also outside the collective. But the kulak was liquidated, the land socialized, and any endeavor to return to private ownership of the soil ruthlessly suppressed. Yes, his freedom was limited to that extent, and tragically so. But his children, born to the collective concept, regard private ownership of land as we would regard private ownership of the air. The child does not have this sense of limitation. The good earth and the life-giving atmosphere are one, he believes. He regards himself as free, as free as any man who has the privilege of influencing the decision of the group. If he is a conscientious objector to collective farming there, he suffers as a conscientious objector to collective killing suffers here.

The American lives on his forty acres, perhaps one hundred sixty; but his products are subject to the market. The price he pays for machinery is not too well related to the price he receives for his produce. Without discussing the steady increase in tenant farming nor the position of the farm laborer, can we say the individualistic farmer is free? The "Okies" were dispossessed, and became the unwanted Western movement of our day. The city summons, and apparently needs, a percentage of farm youth, because the city does not reproduce itself. Studies indicate that the superior, judging by school records, leave the farm. Apparently the freedom is not so attractive as the freedom of the city. The individual farmer must unite with his fellows in associations to provide irrigation, in co-operatives to market his products, but cannot face up to the greater issues of building dams providing flood control and irrigation. Here the people must step in; or, if the private corporation develops the power, it makes its decisions not on what is best for the farmer but on what is best for its stockholders. "Best" may mean quantity at low price, but blindness has dictated too largely scarcity at high price.

I seek to make no case for the collective farm, nor for the private farm. I simply point out that in the one case the man is not completely a slave and in the other he is not entirely a free man. And I have not raised the larger question, What of the interests of the many in the products of the soil. How are we to determine how much wheat, corn, and rye should be produced? Are we to rely upon the mysterious working of the iron laws of the market? Is that the reason for surplus cotton? Was it good sense to turn over grazing land to raise wheat when prices were high—and create a dust bowl? Would such a corporation as the American Telephone and Telegraph Company think it wise to allow each village to determine the kind of equipment it will use, to order on guess the number of phones, to follow old methods because it so desires? No, there is planning on a national scale for the best telephone service for the nation as a whole. Does this end the freedom of the local community? Am I enslaved because I cannot have the old wall telephone and hear my bell ring six times on a party line if I still want to hear the gossip of my neighbors and like the sound of telephone bells? So far as I know, I am not given so much as a vote on the question of change. I happen to own stock in that very company, but as an owner I am not consulted. Yes, I receive notices of annual meetings and requests for proxies, but know that, even if I went there, I could not do much about the matter. Is my freedom gone?

We hear much of regimentation, coupled with pleas for individual initiative and freedom. Closer examination of facts indicates that for the millions there is very little difference between working for the municipally owned power and light and the private power corporation. It is hard to distinguish the differences in the realm of initiative between the worker on the state-owned railway of Alaska or of Panama and the worker on the privately owned Pennsylvania or Union Pacific. The clerk in the chain grocery store or the chain drug store differs how much in liberty from the postman who delivers the mail? Where are these amazing differences? What differentiates the professor in the laboratories of the State University from the professor in Harvard? We forget that capitalism has built up its great bureaucracy, and that research workers of the Bell Telephone laboratories, of General Motors and General Electric work on salaries, are promoted slowly, and possess a certain security, similar to those who work for the Department of Agriculture or the Bureau of Standards. I speak from the standpoint of the man himself. Now, of course, there are areas in which the avenues are open and always will be. A young automobile salesman of exceptional ability, of personal charm, moves from an agency in Los Angeles to sales manager of a large automobile corporation and within a few years is its president. So, too, a young lawyer moves to the head of the Tennessee Valley Authority. But for the masses of men and women, the duties in the teller's cage of the private bank are similar to the duties of the cashier's cage of the tax collector's office. The efficiency of capitalism is based very largely upon large-scale operation, and its efficiency reaches limits at certain size and tends to drop as the unit becomes so large as to carry all of the bureaucratic dangers of centralized state control and ownership. The political menace that accompanies public enterprise is of a piece with the self-interest menace that puts business good before community good, destroys competitors, and moves to monopoly. It is not a matter of paying homage to one and refusing respect to the other. It is, rather, a matter of facing them with open mind and, in the light of the good of the one and of the many, choosing such methods as may give best hope of serving best.

The expression of self lauded by the advocates of free enterprise is less fact than fancy. Punching the clock, working at a particular bolt as it comes along the assembly line, unacquainted with the whole process and but a cog in it, signing for the pay envelope, a number against a name, wage determined in a collective bargain—this is not a picture of a man up before the dawn, shirt sleeves rolled up, cutting down the forest and building a saw mill, tomorrow an industrial captain. No, the piece worker and the time-clock puncher do not worry too much about the plant or the product. They think of the loss of the job and of old age, of their children. Thus, when Utopian proposals come from the dictators, whether to unite and lose chains or obey and rule the world, the worker who knows his freedom is less than political leaders fondly announce turns to the alluring music of contemporary Pied Pipers, often marching to his doom. It is not a long journey from the liveried doorman to the colored-shirted yes man.

There is but one way whereby labor may be changed from the task of servility to the privilege of service, and that is to bring the play of his mind to the process. This calls for the democratic element. The trade unionist, accepting the capitalist system, sees it in the extension of collective bargaining to collective planning of the work; the co-operator sees it in co-operative ownership; the socialist sees it in collective ownership—wherever it may lie, it must be found. Work becomes a spiritual experience and makes possible fullness of life, not only when the product enriches life, but when the producer of the product finds joy in its production.

Again, there is fear that man, freed from the struggle for food and for shelter, relieved of the necessity of obeying a refined law of the jungle called competition, will cease to be creative and that assurance of the satisfaction of physical need will start a process of disintegration, centering in laziness, that eventually will destroy the race. But, no, competition will remain—competition of another sort. It has been called "friendly rivalry in mutual service." I think it will be a little fiercer than that. It will be a competition for recognition by one's fellows, the distinction of doing a better job than others, the distinction of discovering, of creating.

Men will compete for approbation, the appreciation of their fellows. There will be the inner spur that drives men to seek self-approval, self-satisfaction. But men will not compete with their fellows, destroying for greed, denying for privilege. The intellectual energy spent in destructive competition will go to constructive co-operation.

When men are released from the need of spending their major effort in providing the so-called physical necessities, this strength can go to the unending enrichment of the spirit. There is only so much food that can be eaten, so many suits that can be worn; but the needs of the spirit are incalculable—music, art, poetry, engineering, on and on as man moves toward the life of his inner divinity. The improvement of the body, the growth of the mind, the development of the soul—until at last the common man lives at the level of the genius of the day, for the genius of tomorrow is beyond the realm of our present ken—are not too much to envision. The unrealized possibilities of our bountiful earth, of our common humanity, may suggest that Jesus was right when he believed that man would do greater work than did he, and that it was not the easy phrase of a religious seer who summoned us to be perfect. The perfect that will beckon us when we reach the perfect that now summons us will be beyond our present ability to think; but to be perfect is not to sound the alluring chimes of the impossible.

III

Man must make himself subject to his ideal. To bring the physical under his control is insufficient. The ego, ever ready to become sinful selfishness, must, like emotions, be brought under mind. It can be done. My honor does not call for a duel if a man calls me a liar. I check on his statement. Perhaps I did lie. Well and good. Tell the truth. Perhaps he lied. Then I am unharmed. No, I still resent it when a man calls me a liar. I am strongly inclined to knock him down; but I do not, because I do not kick a chair over which I stumble. I never think of sending a second to arrange for weapons and all the little niceties of killing a former friend because he got mad and called me a liar. They call Christ the "Terrible Meek." Yes, the power he wielded was terrible; but I do not like the term. People were not terrified by him. He was the Glorious Gentle, with a gentleness that must become a part of the gentleman.

The fact of inequality is admitted. Some men are tall, and some are short; some possess intelligence quotients that border on genius, and some escape the moron by a narrow margin. Some are born with a song in their hearts, and some possess creative genius and inventive skills. The roll may be called of poet and peasant, of king and pauper, of teacher and student; but does it follow that the drive of poverty is the proper spur to achievement? The leveling down that is predicted may prove to be a leveling up. How many have lost the artist's appreciation of light in the blackness of the coal pit? The soul as well as the body dies when the tuberculosis of the slums seizes its victim. A tall boy reading by the hearth may mean a Lincoln and a Gettysburg Address, but the denial of education more probably means illiterate masses. No, there is another approach; and that is to see the advance that can be made when the socially unnecessary inequalities that root in poor food, poor health, poor housing, and poor clothing are removed. Is it the lack of food that drives the scholar to his task? Does the engineer build our modern miracles of construction because he stands in the bitter cold, inadequately clothed? This is not for a moment to deny that a coddling security may produce the the sluggishly satisfied. Study the privileged. Watch the slow deterioration that sets in where there is no need to labor. The answer lies not in the maintaining the quicksands of inequality but in laying the rocklike foundations through the educational process in which there develops a common acceptance of such concepts as the universal obligation to work. The parasite who does not toil in peace is as reprehensible as the traitor who betrays in war. Living upon the labor of another must become as repugnant as beating a child. The creator must be honored; the man who makes two blades of grass grow where one grew before, extolled. There is drive in social approbation as well as spur in necessity. Let us create the drives that spring from the spirit rather than the stomach.

The claims of individual men and of individual nations to welfare must be equal—just as claims before the law. Rationing is not only a matter of retarding inflation; it is feeding on the basis of personality rather than effective demand. Is there no lesson here? No man shall gorge until all are fed. If we are to be brothers in the future life, why not now? In a new age, doctrine meets doctrine. One or the other survives. But life also meets life. True survival lies in ideas that command and lives that commend. We seek the good man in the good society. Good men are apt to fight a losing fight in a bad society. We must make the conditions under which they wage their warfare as favorable to goodness as is socially possible.

IV

Is the Christian doctrine that love calls forth the second mile or the running of a full course to be discounted? If the heart, strangely warmed by the redeeming love of Christ, is incapable of inciting the will to creative action and to inspiring leadership, our message is vain. We dare not admit that the stern command of poverty is more compelling than the inner compulsion of love. We forget this at our peril.

It is the duty of the many to mark the highways of society with a "No Thoroughfare" sign here to stop the mighty who would march through the lands of the meek, and a sign reading "Dead End Street" there to warn the selfish. This is not to impede traffic. To change the figure, it means that the capacity to corner wheat must not be used to deny bread to the man of reticence and artistic insight lest, lacking bread, he cannot paint.

The Christian and the democrat see the individual as an end. We insist the state is for him. We repudiate the fascist doctrine that he is for the state. While this is clear to us, it is not so clear to our critics. They see the individual as a product of the group and insist that this is as much a fact as is the more evident fact that the group is made of individuals. Salvador de Madariaga, in his *Anarchy or Hierarchy,* sees in liberal democracy forces of anarchy:

> Liberty understood as an absolutely individualistic right and extended to many individuals incapable of administering it, or indifferent to the duties which it implies; equality, felt as a leveling agent, inimicable by instinct to all hierarchy, to all specialization, to all competence, and even to all natural difference; democracy, transformed from the ideal and normative plane of aims to the immediate and empirical plane of methods; capitalism, left free to roam in search of its prey and allowed to fall

back on the State for help when its chase has proved too dangerous; labour, convinced that in it resides the productive power of the nation and resentful of the other classes as despoilers of its own property—all these forces are disruptive, divergent, all work within the State as grave diseases within the body, for all are directed to fostering the interests of individuals or of classes, but not that of the State conceived as an organic whole. Now the mental attitudes of the several classes of society are the soil in which predispositions germinate, and predispositions are the inner conditions which predetermine the actions of men. It is evident, therefore, that liberal democracies evolve in our day under a strong predisposition towards anarchy.[3]

Madariaga points out that the techniques essential to modern government call for the specialist and are beyond the capacity and competence of the ordinary citizen. Man loses control over the state at the very moment the state increases control over him, but he sees the state itself more and more brought under the sway of the uncontrolled powers of industry and finance. Finance capital becomes the dispenser of money by the very fact that deposits in reserve are but a small percentage of deposits in fact, and becomes boss of industry by financing expansion and thus dictating policy. The international ramifications of this control are great. Policies determined by finance within the nation have profound repercussions in other lands, more powerful than those of the state itself.

Human beings are the only real and tangible entities, the only creatures which really do exist and, in whom all spirits and tendencies are manifested. Individual man is the home of liberty, of authority, of anarchy, of dictatorship, of order, of equilibrium, of the health of the State; and as for the nation, where does it

[3] London: George Allen & Unwin, 1937, pp. 47-48.

exist if not in the hearts of its citizens, i.e., separately and completely felt in the heart of every one of the flesh and blood citizens who compose it?

It is not merely that the individual is king, but that he is the only thing there is. There is nothing but individuals, so much so that when from the heights of theoretical discussions we come down to the practical applications of the principles adopted, whatever they may be, we find it all amounts to relations of power between the individual-who-governs and the individual-who-is-goverened, so that authoritarian governments differ from liberal governments in that under the former the individual-who-governs has more liberty, or, in other words, that, in the last resort, authority means liberty of the individual-who-governs.

It is true that these individuals would be less themselves, that they would live a far more elementary and vegetating life were there not institutions to insert them, so to speak, within an ensemble which constitutes a kind of social tissue. But the organic image, which was necessary to correct the mechanical errors of the nineteenth century, is dangerous in that it reduces the individual to the rank of a cell of the body, social or national, which therefore becomes the supreme end to which the individual is but the means. No, one thousand times no. The supreme end is the individual, and collective institutions should have no more hold over him than is needed for his own individual development.

. . . .

[Man is a] higher, wider, deeper concept than Englishman, Frenchman, American, Russian . . . [There is] no more dangerous heresy . . . than that which puts nation above man.

. . . .

What nature gives us is the synthetical fact: the individual-in-society. We call *individual* one of the poles of this living fact; we call *society* the other. When we say *society,* we imply the existence of the individuals which it contains; when we say *individual,* we refer to man precisely as a member of society.

Madariaga assigns finality as an attribute not of the state but of man, and concludes that "the individual cannot be understood without a community"—let us say the state. The state justifies itself only as servant but is "entitled to curtail non-essential liberties to the extent necessary for its own constitution, preservation and working." He then reaches the conclusion that "the citizen is for the State and the State for man." In terms of efficiency, the functional state is justified, he argues, provided that the functional state exists for aims and values in which liberty is the rule and man reigns as master of his own thoughts and destinies.

"Order may be defined as the stable equilibrium between liberty and authority." Here, again, we must realize that this balance is realized only in the individual. "A society enjoys order, if and when a sufficient number of its citizens achieve the balance of liberty and authority in their minds."

So far we have been dealing with these two antagonistic tendencies as we might have discussed the mechanical relations between the two forces of cohesion and dispersion which physicists discriminate in physical bodies. The body politic has also its molecules, men, its force of cohesion, authority, and its force of dispersion, individual liberty. And so that the parallel may be complete, there are political bodies or communities in which authority or cohesion is stronger than liberty or dispersion, and thus they may be compared to solids; others in which liberty prevails over authority, and thus they resemble gases; while there is a middle or balanced type which may be likened to the liquids of physics, in which cohesion and dispersion, authority and liberty, are even. And again, so that our comparison may accompany us all the way and give us assurance to think along the same line, these different states of political communities further resemble the states of matter in that they depend on circumstances; just as in physics heat makes solids pass into liquids and liquids into gases, historical circumstances may solidify the most undisciplined nation into an authoritarian State, only to leave it free to fall back again to its normal ways when the circumstances which had determined the change have passed.

These disquisitions are by no means set down merely as curious or ingenious illustrations; they aim at conveying the relative and movable character of the ideas of liberty and authority which, handled by theoretical and legalistic minds, may have acquired a somewhat rigid and dogmatic aspect. We should envisage liberty not as a goddess, not as a figure of law, not as an abstract idea to be represented by a stone or bronze lady with a torch of the same material emitting dark radiations of nothingness into the void; but as a living tendency, fluid, undetermined, unharnessed, and unshaped, waiting in our living soul to shoot off in a definite form, direction, and intensity whenever a concrete stimulus is forthcoming. We should visualize authority as the tendency antagonistic to liberty, not, again, an abstract notion straight out of a book, but an urge to action and power on the part of a particular man occupying a key position in the State, an urge inextricably mixed with his own tendency to liberty, which happens at the moment to be harnessed by circumstances to the repression of the liberty of others with a view to fitting them into a collective system. For, let us say it again, nothing exists outside individual man and, though the feeling of authority in a community results from the *composition* (in the mathematical sense of the word) of the urge towards authority in all the men of the community, its actual expression in the State takes place through the instrumentality of the particular man or men in office; it manifests itself therefore with the colour, tendency, and intensity which this individual man or these individual men give it out of their own concrete personalities, and participates in the vigour of these concrete personalities, which implies that it participates in the sense of liberty in these men.

Thus understood as tendencies alive and relative, in mutual cooperation and antagonism—in fact, as the two faces of the same medal, the two opposite tensions on the same string—liberty and authority may now be studied in relation to the end of individual life on the one hand and to the function and utility of the State on the other.

. . . .

Our first principle of practical politics will therefore be that liberty need not justify itself; what must be justified at every step is restriction of liberty

. . . .

The higher interests of the individual are coincident with the maximum liberty and the richest experience which he can achieve.[4]

The restraint upon the individual must be reduced to the minimum lest restraint become a straight jacket and the person cease to be free. The government that governs least is the best—so goes the argument. The advocates of the individualism of yesterday took it for granted that man is selfish and will always be selfish, At first it was held that my selfishness will balance your selfishness, that if I take too much from the common pot someone seeking his share will restrain me and that in this interplay of conflicting selfish wills progress will be made: each selfish person will seek to get the better of the other; and, in the competition that follows, I'll produce a better way of making a machine; and thus society benefits. Then, if I rest on my laurels, another man who has suffered from the competition will have thought of a way to improve my process; and before long he gives the improvement to man, and I must be at it again if I am to survive. So on and on it goes, continued progress in a free market, society receiving the benefits of the forced improvements in methods, organization, and service. It never seems to have struck the advocates that the strong

[4] *Ibid.*, pp. 77, 78, 84, 87, 88, 89, 90, 91, 92-94, 95, 98.

might unite, reduce their struggle, and reap the benefits. It was soon revealed that the actual working of the instinct of selfishness was brutal. The social records of the nineteenth century are evidence sufficient. So men talked of "enlightened selfishness." It is like the request for rules of war. When decision rests on self-interest, enlightenment is a secondary matter.

The Christian replies that enlightened selfishness is not the answer. Man must be ruled by love. The strong individual who is subject to love is a safe individual, the strong servant.

But good will in an individual, like love in the heart of a father, may not find the answer. I love my children; yet when the need for surgery arises, I must rely upon men who know, who possess the requisite skill. I turn to them. My love is insufficient. My love for my brother may be all consuming; but if my brother drinks from a polluted stream and dies of typhoid, I find I am dependent upon a group action for the expression of my love. If my brother cannot market his produce, I can do little more than offer sympathy, no matter how deep my love. If in a group I seek with my fellows to express love, my fellows and I may think of the group alone and unconsciously move into the realm of selfishness and advocate policies in the group and for the group that may affect others adversely. All of this means that love, to live, must express itself in terms of knowledge. What we know must be used for the common good. This calls for proper planning, so that free men, working within their respective fields of service, may be contributing to the good of all.

I do not like the figure of the Army, because it suggests regimentation that is repugnant to the present discussion.

But there is a General Staff. Research is done. All of the Army's units are related to one objective. We do not, when training a great number of infantrymen, fail to train the requisite number of airmen. In the Army, of necessity, decisions are made secretly and executed autocratically. Eliminating the elements of secrecy and autocracy, the community reaches decision upon the basis of research made known to its representatives; the fullest publicity is given; the educational facilities of the nation—its free press, radio, and so forth—are to be used to acquaint the people with what can be done. They decide whether it ought to be done. The decision on the great ends is democratic. Again, and within the over-all decision, the execution is carried out in the multiplied units down to the last worker; but within the units, again, the democratic principle is present, the voice of the worker heard when management announces method and policy to attain its goal within the over-all objective.

When we speak of the values of competition, we must turn to the facts. Is there competition in the telephone business of the United States? If we retained private operation, could we assign the telephone service to the American Telephone and Telegraph Company; introduce the democratic element through an expansion of collective bargaining; and maintain stricter control by the political institutions that make the basic decisions for the unit of service, so that it takes its field of service at the request of the community rather than seeking to determine the life of the community in its interest? Or, if we decide that monopoly should be collectively owned, whatever the decision, can we not put the democratic principle to work through the extension of the questions to be decided in the collective-bargain field? And what of the railroads? We found it necessary to exercise control through the Interstate Commerce Commission. When it is said that the control is the reason for the lack of imagination in the pre-war railroad industry of the nation, it is but necessary to study the practices that necessitated the control. The play of self-interest did not make for social good, and rebates granted to destroy competitors and discrimination practiced against sections of the country in order to maintain privileges of financial interests that controlled the railroads were a part of the picture. The financial handling of the New York, New Haven and Hartford, to mention but a single case, is sufficient. Real railroad men, capable and ready to operate the road, were forced to serve the dictates of finance capital whose interest was not primarily efficient operation but efficient appropriation of all the traffic would bear. Is there a case that could be made for overserved sections in the presence of underserved sections? Of course, the difficulty lies in the fact that those who object to planning, who have fought regulation and now call for it to estop planning, are strong. Their voice is heard where decision is made; and the proposals of the people are so modified by the tactics of those whose interest is to discredit, but not to discover, as to be made unworkable. Whatever may be the answer, there is conflict of interest between the individual, and organized individuals, who move upon the basis of greed and the community whose major interest is, naturally, common good.

VI

The planning suggested here, democratic, growing out of need, seeking the fullest freedom of the person consonant with the freedom of the people, has been discussed on a national basis. But it cannot rest here. Just as planning by the producer or the consumer will not do—it must be by all—planning by one nation will not do. Common-good planning by the people must supplant special-privilege planning by the cartel. A nation's acts in terms of tariff, currency, and so forth, have far-reaching effects. No follower of Jesus can justify a decision to benefit workers here that will dislocate the economy of a nation there and bring its workers to starvation and revolution. There must be over-all planning in terms of the whole world. "Impossible," "Too vast," it is said. I think not. The public-health experts will find it no more difficult to apply their knowledge upon a world basis than upon a national basis. Typhus is typhus wherever found. Sulphas are effective in Persia and in Hawaii. The research of the laboratories of the East and the West, and of black man and white man, are available for all men and can be applied to protect men everywhere. Regulations relative to quarantine, purity of water and of drugs, to mention but a few, can be established upon a world basis. The planning can be done. It is then a matter of carrying down the agreed plans to the nation, the community, the person.

We are one. We can plan as one. When the wife of the late Bishop Frederick Bohn Fisher took an Indian child up in her arms, she did not know that the burning body of the child was tortured by typhus; but three days later she was dead. Her heart-broken husband wrote the tribute for the stone that marks her resting place: "She died serving." The planning that unites the interests of the one and the many will be wrought under the motto, "They lived serving."

The concept of the many must include all. Perhaps it would be better to speak of the one and the all. The many may indicate a class, a nation, a race. Generally we think of the nation, and the many indicate the collective aspect of the community—the state. The one and the many cannot be harmonized at the national level. Religion has made this clear. It was the world that was on the heart of Jesus; it was the world for which he died; it was the world to which God sent his Son. There follows the necessity not only of balancing the needs of the individual and the needs of his national community but of extending the balance until equilibrium shall have been reached between the individual and the world itself. Equilibrium must not be thought of as being at rest. The needs of the individual at times thrust against the demands of the community, and vice versa. There will be a slight roll of the ship of state, but not one great enough to capsize it. World patriotism, certainly world consciousness, is demanded for this balance. The contribution of religion to world-mindedness has been significant. It is revealed in the basic doctrines of Christianity, mainfest in its missionary movement, and ever present in its vision of a redeemed humanity.

The community is also dependent upon the freedom not alone to investigate but to publicize the investigation. Sidney and Beatrice Webb have called for measurement and publicity as prime essentials. The scientific study is seen in the term "measurement"; the full expression of the findings of the people is seen in the term "publicity."

Madariaga is wrong in assuming that the anarchial tendencies inherent in the free groupings of men characteristic of democratic society—such as the churches and the teachers' organizations, the trade unions and the businessmen's associations, literary groupings and political parties—are dominant. That such tendencies exist is admitted; but the freedom that lies in these groupings, expressing at times proper and determined criticisms of the activities of the state, constitutes the checks and balances that protect the liberty of the individual and, in the long run, gives stability to the state. Dictatorship not only decapitates its opposition but, in coercing, destroys the creative mind. We must beware of any policy that estops creative research. For instance, the education during the period of war has been but an application of present knowledge to a specific need. Creative research has been in large measure restricted. Thus, during the period of conflict no new knowledge has come to man. He has but applied what he knows. There is a halt in the march into new knowledge. This we regard as temporary. Under the dictator it takes on permanence. The creative mind is forced into the applied field. The creator must work in harmony with predetermined principles.

Eternal vigilance is the price of liberty. The vigilance that must be exercised, however, is a two-faced creature. It must be capable of looking upon the activities of the individual who, moving to power, controls other individuals and thus denies them liberty because he is powerful enough to control the state. The group must be on the alert lest the state lose its liberty. It must be equally on the alert lest its own activities in protecting the state should erect a monster that in turn destroys the liberty of the individual. There is no sufficient reason why man cannot strike a proper balance between the interests of the one and the many, provided he possesses a common faith and a common purpose that is dynamic. The world faith of Christianity calls for a world purpose, one expression of which is the co-ordinating of national economy and world economy.

Men who know what they want are more likely to get what they want. What we want is a matter of faith. In all the statement and restatement of Christian principle, careful examination will allow one to say: Here is insistence upon the dignity of man, the informing principle of democracy; here is the affirmation of brotherhood, the essential objective of the group; here is the exaltation of love, the cohesive factor upon which social unity rests; here is the validation of comradeship, the fact of one family to which every human being belongs; here is the assurance of life eternal, the realization that we are living forever now; here is the revelation of the ideal in a person, the Leader, our Lord and Saviour, to whom absolute obedience is due and from whom utter satisfaction is pledged. Such a faith eventuates in a purpose. It commandeers the intelligence and the will of man, his scientific achievements, his culture, the institutions he has created, his factories, the natural resources with which God has blessed him—all to be used for the one supreme objective of enriching the personality of every individual to the end that each person shall have full opportunity to move from the limitations of humanity to the expressions of potential divinity. Men who give allegiance to such a faith will be the first to recognize their sinfulness and the need of salvation. Such persons may experience the love of God, and, in accepting that love and in giving their all to do his will, may reach the inner assurance that enables them to press on to the goal of high calling, constantly realizing their own imperfections but hearing forever the command, "Be ye therefore perfect."

Man will not forget the gains of the past as he contemplates the greater gain of the future. He will remember that, when feudalism was superseded by capitalism, the individual who had been attached to the soil, who gave service for protection and thus received a certain degree of security, was freer than the slave who was owned, yet was not completely free because his labor belonged to his overlord. It was not his own. When the capitalist entrepreneur offered him a wage for his labor, it was his labor. He sold it where he liked, to whom he liked. This was his right. He was more of an individual than he was as a serf. He, a person, contracted with another person. He was free to contract, free to refuse. He learned also that no priest was necessary to represent him before God. He could be free from the authority of the Church, a Protestant, who could follow the dictates of his own conscience rather than be ruled by the mandates of the priest. And if he could work for whom he pleased, serve God as he pleased, he would, by all that was holy, think as he pleased. The rights of man were affirmed. He was an individual. He had existed as a bound member of a group, slave or serf. Now he was a free citizen and would be a member of a group by contract. Professor Hocking writes:

A man's ultimate relations are solely to God; and perhaps the deepest thing in Christianity is the adequacy with which it presents this ultimate solitude of the soul, not alone in birth and in death, but in the history of its own ethical problem, which no one can meet for it. This is the essential freedom of the self, that it stands for a fateful moment outside of all belongings and determines for itself alone whether its primary attachments shall be with actual earthly interests or with those of an ideal and potential "Kingdom of God." Individuality is not a fixed membership, as of an organ in an organism, but a continued living tension between various possibilities of belonging. . . . The modern individual is thought of as having a comprehensive set of "rights" or "owns"—his *own* conscience, his *own* occupation and property, his *own* enterprise, his *own* opinions, his *own* vote, his *own* chance for office.[5]

Hocking sees a revolution in the question of the serf, "Whose man shall I be?" Heretofore that question was not asked. It marked the march from the formula "to every group, numerous men and sets of men" toward the formula "to every man, numerous groups and possible groups." Is it not possible to retain the latter—to every man, numerous groups and possible groups—and at the same time to insure that to the nation-group, the world-group, numerous men and sets of men, whose conceptions of service necessitate loyalty to the group as well as demand opportunity within the group?

Thus individualism stresses rights. Its life depends upon an equal stressing of duty. Rights disassociated from morality and social obligations are dangerous. The expression of such rights does not make for social unity. Is it to be believed that each unit of modern enterprise, making its own decision in its own interests, can give us a common answer to the common question of what shall be produced in this land? The obligation of duty has not been a part of the insistence upon rights in individualism. Some question that it can be as long as the basic decision is in the field of self-interest. The interests of the one and the many are in large measure reconciled when a common purpose emerges from a common faith, and the individual, giving himself to the common pur-

[5] W. E. Hocking, *The Lasting Elements of Individualism* (New Haven: Yale University Press, 1937), pp. 22-23.

pose, expresses his personality in a service that contributes to the purpose and therefore serves the many. And the many, by adhering to the common purpose, a purpose that is moral because born of faith, contribute to the one because it is in the interests of the many that the one should reach full-statured personality.

Here, as in religion everywhere, the action of the one and the action of the many must spring from good will whose primary stimulus is love. Is this to be Utopian? Is this to speak of the absolute in simple terms and be deaf to the warning that human nature does not change, that the proposal is doomed since the possible relative measure in history is far from the ideal, so far that the one and the many really remain in conflict? Not at all; it is but a challenge to a preacher in a revolutionary age to announce and to enthrone the redemptive and reconciling principle of his faith, the love that can unite law and liberty, the love that of itself is the principle of unity in which the principle of change and the principle of stability may serve the individual and the group in reciprocal contribution.

CHAPTER IV

THE PREACHER IN A REVOLUTIONARY AGE

In a revolutionary era, as in all other ages, the preacher traces sin to its consequences. The preacher believes we live in a moral universe. Thus, he seeks to discover and declare the moral law. In the long history of preaching, the religious thinker has learned to evaluate alternatives. Consequences flow from choices. "This do, and thou shalt live." Whether evil be done by Macbeth or a modern madman, the preacher knows that Duncan's death is forever followed by Macduff's retribution. It simply is not done, "when 'tis done." Now, as then,

> False face must hide what the false heart doth know.

Does the contemporary Macbeth ask:

> Will all great Neptune's ocean wash this blood
> Clean from my hand?

The answer is written into the nature of things:

> No, this my hand will rather
> The multitudinous seas incarnadine,
> Making the green one red.

True preaching declares truth that is timeless. The preaching of a revolutionary age is, therefore, less a matter of current calendar than of continuing centuries.

True enough, some preaching is dated. Its exponents are but wooden Charlie McCarthys voicing the views of contemporary Bergens, protesting the poor pay but content to sit upon the knee of the masters whose voice they are. True preachers proclaim the unsearchable riches of God in the name of a Master who was the way, the truth, and the life.

It is the speech of the prophet that must be heard in the pulpit of the free. It must be declaratory of the will of God: "Thus saith the Lord"—the affirmation of the moral law, the principles of conduct. It must be the speech of judgment: "Thou art the man." It must be the speech heralding the new day: "The kingdom of God is at hand"; "Let justice roll on as a flood of waters, and righteousness like an unfailing stream." It must be the speech of accusation: "They sell the righteous for money, and the needy for a pair of shoes." It must be clear and courageous speech. The prophet is done with anonymity when the holy name is profaned in act more blasphemous than words: "Upon garments taken in pledge they stretch themselves beside every altar, and the wine of those who have been fined they drink in the house of their God"; [1] "Alas, for those who turn judgment to wormwood, and cast down righteousness to the ground, who hate him that reproves in the gate, and abhor one that speaks uprightly!" A leisure class has no place in a working society: "They who lie on ivory couches, and sprawl upon their divans, and eat lambs from the flock, and calves from out the stall; they drawl to the sound of the lyre; . . . they drink bowlfuls of

[1] Amos 2:8 according to Charles Foster Kent, *The Student's Old Testament* (Charles Scribner's Sons, 1910).

wine, and anoint themselves with the finest of oil, but they do not grieve over the ruin of Joseph." [2] This speech was understood. Amaziah knew what Amos was driving at. It was his judgment that "the land is not able to bear all his words." The preacher in revolutionary days must speak of imperialism and injustice, of exploitation, of world order and equality and creative service—and the land may not be able to bear all his words. He must speak of sin where sin is—the place may be high or low.

Several years ago I was invited to deliver an address in the New York Stock Exchange. I was presented to its president, and during our conversation I said: "I have always wanted to stand on the floor of the exchange. I wonder if I may." The president replied: "I am sorry, very sorry; but we have passed a rule recently that forbids anyone to go on the floor except members and employees. You see, we have received many threatening notes from communists; the rule is one for self-protection and is rigidly enforced." It was not many months after that meeting that I saw a newspaper picture of that man, no longer president of the New York Stock Exchange, but a prisoner of the State of New York, handcuffed to other prisoners and en route to Sing Sing. My sympathy went out to him and his family, as it would to any man in trouble; but I knew that the real menace to American institutions was less the threat of revolutionaries without than the presence of sin within. Preaching must be more than the voice of judgment; it must be the summons to salvation. It must call to repentance but offer redeeming love. The preacher must not be fearful of tracing sin to its conse-

[2] Amos 6:4-5, 6, *ibid.*

quences, nor of predicting the certain results of social sinning. Amos declared: "Behold the eyes of the Lord Jehovah are upon the sinful kingdom, and I will destroy it from the face of the earth. . . . It is the oracle of Jehovah." The preacher must know, as Hosea knew, that the people are but as their priestlings. It is the love that Jehovah delights in and not sacrifice, knowledge and not burnt offerings. The note of love must be spoken. Poor Hosea, did he not know the meaning of love rejected and love requited? He cannot preach doom alone; forgiveness follows love: "Return, O Israel, to Jehovah thy God; for thou hast stumbled through thine iniquity. . . . Return to . . . thy God."

The call to penitence, the prayer for pardon, the offer of mercy, the love that seeks to save, must be at the forefront of preaching. How little it is that is required and how much —justice, mercy, humility! Prophetic utterance must never be divorced from the message of redemption—the justice of God, yes; but the grace of God, always.

I

Not long after my election to the episcopacy, I shared certain impressions, under the theme "Some Negatives from the Candid Camera of a New Bishop," with a few of my ministerial colleagues. Since the kind of preaching a revolutionary age will hear is determined by the kind of preacher who occupies the pulpit, I reshare those impressions here. Several years ago I bought a Leica. The mechancial perfection of this amazing camera captivates one; and after a time the novice hesitatingly refers to "range finder," "methods of focusing," "the coincidence of images," and speaks of "time" and of "light." Candid photography deals with negatives.

The expert prints only the good ones; but a beginner like me must print all, the good and the bad. I carried this practice of printing good and bad over into this report of some mental photography. The shots have been candid, and I share with you a few prints.

From the college presidency to the episcopacy is in many ways a transition from ivory tower to circus tent. Of course, no college is an ivory tower; and the episcopacy is not entirely a circus. But being a bishop does involve lion taming. Bishops are called upon to face the shining teeth and awful roars of lionlike committees who insist that the new minister must have the ability of Harry Emerson Fosdick, must not be over twenty-eight years of age, and should start at the substantial sum of $1200 and house. Then, of course, there is not a little tightrope walking. The balancing stick supplants the shepherd's crook. It might be wiser to come down upon one side or the other of an issue rather than to remain aloft as the perfect symbol of balance. A bishop must have the ability to manage the occasional clown, check up on the jugglers and sleight-of-hand performers, and be certain that the sideshows do not outshine the performance in the main tent. The episcopacy, like the circus, is an itinerant undertaking. There is much setting up of tents and moving from town to town. I must not forget the merry-go-round. To sounding brass and tinkling cymbal, a bishop, clad in purple, mounts his horse, all too often getting off at the spot where he mounted, sometimes clutching the gold ring heroically won as the wooden horse rushed by. But it is not the circus aspect of the episcopacy I would discuss; I would present a few prints from the candid shooting of a new bishop.

The first picture bears a strange title. Unless you are a motion-picture devotee, the caption may prove meaningless. I would like to call this negative "Step'nfetchit." You are acquainted, I trust, with the ambling Negro who bears this name. A few years ago he was prominent in the pictures. You will recall him as the Negro who had the emptiness of the ages in his face and the laziness of the centuries in his whines. His conversation was a monotonous cross between a moan and a mumble. In a scene from a play of ten years ago Step'nfetchit finds himself in Paris just before the first World War begins. He has come from New Orleans. He is there with his employer. War is declared. He stands in awe, watching the columns of marching men. He does not know what it is all about but is captivated by the colorful uniforms and the singing. Finally, he sees some French soldiers from Morocco. They are Negroes dressed in the uniform of Africa —great pantaloons of brilliant red, bright tunics, red turbans, shoes with turned-up toes. Sep'nfetchit is drawn like a moth to a flame. Such clothes! And Negroes, too! He falls in step and addresses the Moroccan soldiers. They stare at one another. They reply in French. They call for an interpreter, but who can interpret Step'nfetchit? He wants a suit like theirs. He thinks they belong to a lodge. He tells them that he was the Most Exalted of the Exalted Mosts of New Orleans. He will join. He will do anything. They shake their heads. They do not understand. Finally, a great idea strikes him. He takes the turban from the head of one of the soldiers and puts it on his own head. The French crowd explodes. "Ah! The brave American! He would fight for La Belle France!" The French cheer. They sing the Marseillaise. With a soldier on either side, Step'nfetchit marches off to a recruiting station. He enlists. He thinks he is joining a lodge. Soon they are at the front. Step'nfetchit thinks this is the greatest initiation he has ever experienced. Now they are in action. Step'nfetchit and his company are in a graveyard. The Germans are coming. Giant guns roar. Boy, what an initiation! Then a whine and an explosion. We hear Step'nfetchit cry, "Say, you all, this lodge is some lodge all right; but if you boys don't look out, somebody's going to get hurt around here." The Germans can be seen crossing No Man's Land. A French corporal yells to Step'nfetchit, "Are you there, America?" Step'nfetchit is in a hole. He stays in it; but he raises his hand to wave to the corporal. His hand is above the protecting ledge of earth. A whistle becomes a shriek joined by a second shriek, and Step'nfetchit stares at a hand with a hole in it. Step'nfetchit thought he was joining a lodge. Actually, he was in a war.

My pictures show a number of men who think they are ministers. Actually, the prints reveal something else.

There is the man who thinks he is a minister but who is really a high-pressure, boisterous, back-slapping, hand-shaking salesman. He is a politician gone religious. He has no sense of refinement. He does not know that light travels faster than sound. Kenneth Fearing has described him in his attempt to portray a high-pressure salesman:

And wow he died as wow he lived,
going WHOOP to the office and BLOOIE home to sleep, and BIFF got married and BAM had children and OOF got fired.
ZOWIE did he live, and ZOWIE did he die.[3]

[3] From "Dirge," in *Poems* (New York: Dynamo, 1935). Used by permission of the author.

He does not know the place of silence in the development of the soul. We are bullied by sound. We develop the anesthesia of inattention, but the shock occurs. We need to know that when we stand still we regain our equilibrium. This man is a promoter, not a priest. He suffers from aprosexia. That is a term that indicates a lack of power to concentrate the mind. He reveals flickering attention. In words of the camera expert, he "panorams" too much. There is too much "movie," to much "talkie." He possesses a split-second mind. Of course, we need aggressive leadership; but this need not be divorced from the cultural, the spiritual, from poise and dignity. This man seldom knows what he creates; he is the man who leaves the debt behind. A Negro was asked what was the cause of the last depression, and his answer was, "I guess the white folks just bought more than they could pay for." It might be well for this man to hear the remark of Whistler, the artist. He took the poor canvas of a student and heard the student say, "I cannot paint what I see." Whistler replied, "Your trouble, my son, is to begin when you see what you paint."

Then there is another picture. We may entitle this "The Professional." He is a job-conscious, highly trained professional, a master of religious ceremony, basically cynical though often a delightful fellow, a gentleman who looks out for his own interests in the job of serving the Lord. Religion is largely a matter of form. This professional expounds Christianity but really accepts the philosophy of George M. Cohan in one of his musical comedies, "When you're rich, you're the smoke; and when you're broke, it's a joke." The pen is mightier than the sword, that is, when it is writing checks. I know of one minister whose father was a minister. His father served sacrificially and laid foundations upon which the great Church has been built. He was a sacrificial servant. His son in the theological school said, "None of that for me. I am looking out for myself." He *has* looked out for himself, and he holds a great pulpit today. It is not for me to question his sincerity. I am eager that all of our work be done perfectly. But when a man has a job instead of a calling, no matter how well he does it, professionalism destroys the spirit. The man I refer to receives a large salary, but it is not alone the occasional professional in the big church to whom I refer. He has a brother, a man of lower talent but one whose outlook is the same.

There is another brother who might be called "The Gossip." Space does not permit a record of this print. The face is somewhat hidden behind a hand. The Gossip is whispering to a layman, "Yes, he's a wonderful fellow, but he can't preach." The broadcast of our gospel is doomed by the interference of the static called unbrotherliness.

But it is not these pictures that I would emphasize. There is another. It is of such a man as I find in the large percentage of our churches, great and small. We may entitle this "The Called Messenger." He is sustained by a sense of being called, driven by the spirit of Christ, seeking naught save the privilege of serving, losing his life and finding it, the devoted slave of the suffering Christ, bearing in his heart and on his body the scars that speak. The Called Messengers! These men impress me. They are like Paul: "I was not disobedient unto the heavenly vision." Paul might have rationalized the whole situation and used his brains to write a thesis on "The Genesis of the Elements Used in the Eucharist in the Light of Pharisaic Ceremonialism"; but, no, he preferred the road that led to Rome. These men know that victory equals will. They strike as concentrated wholes. They are not divided personalities. They have entered our work in a way that reveals the truth of what Marcianus said to Augustine: "This day that brings another life to thee demands that thou another man must be."

The Called Messengers carry on; they see history as a strange pendulum that swings from the acceptance of the rejected to the rejection of the accepted. They seem to know, as did Jesus, "My Father worketh hitherto, and I work." They have seen the long struggle up through the fighting way of life, the money-making way of life. They are stable when others crack up. They do not turn to cynical defeatism. They turn neither to the left of communism, insisting that we note the red rash upon their chests, nor to the right of fascism, with sleeves rolled up to show the muscles of the brute. Nor do not turn to the compensating aspects of religion. As I have studied these men, they appear to have met the Eternal, to have learned that they are co-workers with the Moral Purpose at the heart of things. Hence they are effective in a revolutionary hour. They would surround men with proper environment, certainly; but they know Christianity was an experience at the beginning. Later, men explained the experience, and now spend too much of their time on the explanation rather than in recreating the experience. They know full well that it is not enough to sing, as we sang a little while ago, "Happy days are here again." Too many people forget that we must also sing, "O wash my soul from every sin, and make my guilty conscience clean." Like the nightingale who "hands on his song from father to son," as Robert Bridges so beautifully puts it, "unchanging to the changeful generations of men," they would give the story of God's redeeming love to men that all may live. These men, as I see them, seek to incarnate the message of our God. They know that Jesus did it. They, the Called Messengers of the Messenger of our God go out to preach the redeeming message, a message that will yet redeem mankind.

Yes, there are pictures of men who call themselves ministers and aren't. There are Professionals. There are Gossips. But they are few as compared with the Called Messengers seen in the honest photography of a new bishop.

II

It is the preaching of the Called Messenger that the revolutionary day eagerly awaits and desperately needs. A few years ago Dr. A. A. Berle, Jr., now assistant secretary of state, was discussing the question of freedom and property. He began by referring to the classic French judgment to the effect that democracy will collapse when it deals with economic problems. Mr. Berle went on to show that, in our thinking, liberty has been associated with property. This was natural in the period following feudalism because men had to have property in order to be free. Men held that freedom of speech and of worship were related to the freedom and right to own property. But the property considered was possessory property. It was something a man could really own, could handle, could work with. The free man who owned a farm and owned his tools could apply tool to land by labor and earn his living. He could work the land and was ready to defend it. Then came the rise of modern banking, the corporation, and contemporary practices of finance capital. Paper property—that is, ownership evidenced by stock certificate or a loan gauranteed by a bond—came into prominence. Paper property rose from 18 per cent of the total in 1900 to 40 per cent in 1937. In the depression of the first decade of the twentieth century, there was sufficient possessory property for the owner to pull in his belt and live upon the soil. But in 1929 this was impossible. A stock certificate cannot be farmed. A bond cannot be irrigated. Dr. Berle went on to show that the government was forced to take responsibility for the economics of the country. He added, that there is a lot of nonsense about economic laws. Adam Smith who formulated these laws did not face this economy. Every one of them can be violated, given a violent enough form of government. The limitations are simply the efficiency of the people and the extent of natural resources. The economic level can be handled, but at the expense of the liberty of the people. "Our essential problem," he said, "is this: Can we get the benefits of centralized economics without losing our liberty?" We see at times that people can do things if they really want to do them. Under the desire to protect the nation in time of war, we do things contrary to these laws. "The result is," he stated, "I have come to the conclusion that we must have an overmastering moral ideal." Such an ideal, if overmastering, will assure us that those possessing freedom will not abuse it; and with such an assurance we can move. The freedom of democracy must be restrained or controlled by its spiritual ideals. Mr. Berle summed it up in a startling conclusion: "The future needs more practicing saints than practical politicians." Preaching must produce them.

The moral ideal Mr. Berle demands is essential, not only for society, but for the individual. The warring interests in the group life are, in different form, present in the individual. Unifying principles are as essential to the person as to the body politic. It becomes apparent, therefore, that preaching takes on major importance. If the Protestant pulpit is dependent upon the civil liberties of democracy for its freedom, it is equally true that democracy is dependent upon the pulpit for those overmastering ideals that will insure that people given freedom will not abuse it. In a day of basic transition it is imperative that democracy possess stable citizens, individuals whose emotions are controlled by ideals enabling them to face the outer storm with inner calm.

One of the most interesting features of modern ships is provision for proper stabilization to eliminate the rolling of the vessel and insure comfort at sea. It is said by those who know that the rolling motion of the ship is the result of fluid pressure acting on the hull and the shifting of that pressure from one side to the other. Waves do not break against a ship the way they do against a solid breakwater. A ship is free to rise and fall. The bulk of each wave passes underneath her, imparting a comparatively light roll before it goes on down the wind. A single wave can only start the rolling. It takes a whole succession of waves to build up a violent rolling motion, each wave adding its push, just as a child gets up momentum on a swing. The problem of the stabilizer, it would therefore appear, is but to counteract the force of the single wave. It will be readily understood that a comparatively small artificial force, equal and opposite to the disturbing increment of each wave and applied at the instant the latter starts, will be sufficient to quench the wave's effect upon the ship. The success of the gyrostabilizer, then, lies in its ability to deal with beginnings; and since beginnings are small, the forces necessary to counteract them are also small. For this reason a ship is never subjected to heavy strains and stresses when the stabilizer is in operation. Preaching ought to supply man with stabilizing equipment. Many thoughtful men believe that individuals and society are doomed without the ideal. If we who preach are the possessors of the necessary ideals, we dare not be recreant to our high trust.

The ministry becomes a socially necessary profession, even in the thought of the irreligious, since it furnishes the overmastering ideal upon which the stable state and the balanced person depend. And the preacher thereby becomes worthy of the title "Reverend"—repugnant now to sensitive men aware of their unworthiness, but earned at last because in such service the preacher is revered by the people.

If the revolutionary epoch is to be marked by advance from competitive struggle to co-operative endeavor, from selfish nationalism to sensible internationalism, from religion grounded in authority to religion based on experience; if the present fearful struggle of the fratricidal sons of Cain is to be followed by the freeing service of the fraternizing sons of Christ; if economic problems that cry aloud for solution are to be solved by overcoming the selfishness that secretly destroys the formulae of reconstruction; if the cynicism and pessimism that make our souls septic are to be overcome by the antiseptic of faith; certainly the preacher must bring, as never before, the law, the prophets, and the gospel in a message that presents truthfully and fearlessly the nemesis that pursues sin, but also persistently and persuasively the message of the new life that follows forgiveness and that moves toward perfection. Yes, the All-Powerful is the All-Loving too. Sin destroys, but love saves. The Great Law-Giver is also the Great Forgiver.

III

No Time for Comedy is the title of a scintillating play marvelously done some years ago by Katherine Cornell and Francis Lederer. The laughter of joy is silenced in an atmosphere of pessimism. One of the characters is a playwright. His wife, in criticizing one of his new plays, says, "I feel a revulsion from your play altogether because it is dominated by the idea of death."

"But," he breaks in, "we are living in an era of death. We are pervaded by death. Death is our hero, our protagonist—war and death—death and the fear of death. Death purrs over us, a giant bombing plane—its shadow over the green pastures, darkening the still waters."

The preacher dare not see the shadow over the green pastures without remembering the table prepared in the presence of enemies. The still waters are darkened, but "the Lord is my shepherd."

We need the faith essential to laughter, but it must not be the laughter of the monastic who has withdrawn in safety from the struggle. S. N. Behrman, in the play I have quoted, has a character say: "It's all right to laugh under fire—that's courage—but not sitting on the side lines—that's callousness." I am certain that preaching in a revolutionary age must revitalize the faith. Too many proclaim it as a matter of professional duty. It must regrip us. It must become faith in fact, not a pretty bit of ritual to be read properly by the gowned functionary whose soft voice subdues the ethical demand "Follow me." It must be a faith that will enable us to stand the shattering blows of existence. Do our pronouncements lack contagion because they did not "take" in our own lives?

In San Francisco a few short years ago I stood beside the bed of my friend Walter John Sherman. His right side was paralyzed. He could not speak, save for the word "No." It was but yesterday I met him for the first time in a little classroom at the Boston University School of Theology, the one with the seats that must have come from an old-fashioned schoolhouse. Lauress J. Birney was in the professor's chair. It was the class in practice preaching, and "Jack" preached. A critical class became a seeking congregation. We heard passionate preaching that day, exquisitely phrased, pleading that reached our hearts. Dean Birney, with tears in his eyes, dismissed us without a word. That was the beginning of a friendship that deepened through the years. He became my closest and dearest friend. I stood beside his bed, in a rebellious mood, knowing that he would never preach again. He reached his left hand toward me. His face lighted up. He seemed to draw strength from that handclasp. What could I say? No meaningless platitudes would do. Here was my friend, silent; and I knew that liars with raucous voices would broadcast from the capitals across the sea, but Jack would speak no more. What about my own faith? What of yours? I told him that the trees of New England were in color again, that from the sky Massachusetts spread out like a rich Oriental rug. I spoke of Lynn and his old church. I knew that I must leave in but a few minutes. He followed every word—and laughed, it seemed at times. But when I came to go, he thought what I thought. He said, "No, no." There was a pause. "No," he repeated. Then, mastering himself, he waved. We had journeyed through Europe together. We hated dictatorship together. I stood at the foot of the bed, a bit nearer the door. Remembering the thousands with their raised-fist salute in Russia, I lifted my arm and, with clenched fist, gave that salute we had seen together. He laughed and lifted his left arm in a *"Heil,* Hitler" gesture. And so I left him, with a half smile upon his face. I stopped outside the door. I had heard a sob, which in heart-breaking crescendo rose to a cry. I walked down the hall. I could hear him when I bowed to the nurse at the desk.

I want a faith that will enable me to carry on when I see my dearest friend, so useful, so talented, sentenced to silence. We need a faith that will enable us to move beyond that age-old problem of evil, beyond the ancient question "Why do the righteous suffer?" on in service until at last man builds a Kingdom for God. Jesus had such faith. And in Jesus I find the overmastering ideal the century needs.

Preaching in a revolutionary era needs more than faith. If in this century the group is resolved to make the externals minister to the essentials; if as a group we are going to do for all what few in religious circles have sought in service to do for a few; if we are to move up from the fighting way of life, beyond the money-making way of life, into an order that may be called the personality-making way of life; if we realize that men who have been trained to compete for self-interest will not do in an order that demands co-operation in the interests of the common good; if the engineer, economist, and executive are to take the ethical ideals and enthrone them in concrete reality; if we are to work out some splendid synthesis whereby the creative initiative that flowed from American individualism is preserved and the benefits that lie in collective action appropriated; then it becomes obvious and imperative that the preacher who serves in a revolutionary age must possess a preparation and a devotion akin to the scholars and the saints who in similar ages have been at once militant and meek, faithful and triumphant.

IV

It was my privilege to study under a remarkable philosopher, a man who wrote no books. He tried to teach students to think. He was an old man, stooped and gray. His eyes were keen, his hair long, his jaw firm, and his lips tender. His pedagogy might be subject to criticism in these days. Strangely enough, he thought it wiser to read what a philosopher had said than to study the critical exposition of a philosopher's thought by someone else. His method was unique. He would say, "Oxnam, stand up. Turn to page 24. Read." I was called upon to read a passage from some thinker—Plato, perhaps. I would read a few lines. "Stop!" the old man would say. Then, "What did he say?" If I had caught the meaning, the old man would say, "Right! Sit down." But if not—and more often it was not—he would say, "Wrong. Read it again." Sometimes a helpful, though not too direct, suggestion; but we stood until we had caught the meaning. I loved that old man. He loved us, but he did not wear his heart on the sleeve of his academic gown. Just before leaving for Boston to enter the theological seminary, I summoned up a bit of courage and asked the old man a question in private: "Dr. Hoose, what advice would you give a young man entering the ministry?" He puckered up his lips; his eyes flashed; there was a moment of silence. "Scholarship, no mannerisms." He turned and walked away, dragging his weary old feet down the hall. I was disappointed. Just three words, "Scholarship, no mannerisms." The next day I was at the Southern Pacific station. My father and mother, my brothers and sister, were there, and, of course, some friends. We were about to say good-by when through the doorway of that station came the old man. Stooped, yes; gray, yes. The long hair tousled out from the big black hat he always wore. He came up and greeted us. Then he pulled me aside and said almost gruffly: "Oxnam, I want to change the advice I gave you last night. I want to add a word: Scholarship, sympathy, no mannerisms." And there it is, and I give it to the younger men who are to preach in a revolutionary age—scholarship, sympathy, no mannerisms.

By recommending scholarship I do not mean to plead for the overspecialized research that sometimes leads to the doctorate. There is a lot of exalted crossword-puzzle activity that labels itself research. This is not to condemn true research, which is the precondition of progress; it is to decry the sterile turning of musty pages for no other purpose than personal satisfaction. The preacher, by reason of his very task, cannot give his life to the mastery of a field of learning, in the sense in which the scholar-specialist must. I have grave doubt about the contribution graduate study beyond the theological course makes to the minister. There is danger that too long a separation from human beings and their struggles may result in permanent estrangement. Our calling is so high that there cannot be too great an intellectual preparation, but it is a calling that calls for equal preparation of the heart. There are some who become so enamored of the library that they are unattracted by the parish.

Perhaps Orozco, the revolutionary artist of Mexico, had

this in mind when he painted in a single night one of the extraordinary murals in the Baker Library at Dartmouth. Lying upon a gigantic delivery table is a colossal mother skeleton. The table is made of ancient books, tremendous tomes. The attending obstetrician is a skeleton clad in an academic gown with appropriate mortarboard. He has just delivered a tiny skeleton and holds it in his hands with meticulous care. The little skeleton wears a mortarboard too. In the foreground are glass jars; and in each jar is a tiny skeleton wearing a mortarboard, stillborn ideas delivered from the gigantic mother skeleton, the university. In the immediate background are several figures, each a skeleton, each clad in academic garb, each wearing a hat or cap signifying the educational institutions of the world. Behind them, in flaming red, are the fires of a world in revolution. Dead theses, delivered by a dead obstetrician, from a dead mother, when the world is aflame! Orozco is not ridiculing research. He is pleading for the creative use of knowledge.

Years ago I was called upon to deliver an address in South India. I was informed that what I said would be taken down in "shorthand." I was amazed when upon reaching the platform I looked down and saw directly before me a man seated behind a table with his back toward me, facing the audience. In front of him was a semicircle made up of ten or twelve tables. At each table sat a man facing the one whose back was toward me. This individual had a long bamboo pole in his hand. When I started to speak he struck the first table on the right with the pole and that man began to write. When I had spoken perhaps four or five sentences he struck the second table and that man turned furiously to his task. And so on he went, striking each table in turn. When he had reached the twelfth table the first man had completed the initial task and his table was struck again, and so on it went in disconcerting efficiency throughout the address. Then the reports were assembled. To my very great surprise, I received a copy that was as accurate as the average stenographic report at home. We live in an hour of necessary specialization. We learn too much at too great speed for any one person to carry on research in all of the fields of modern learning. But specialization, unless balanced by "seeing things whole," leads to bedlam. There is need for assembling the knowledge of men for such interpretation as will give men understanding of the universe—a world view, as we say. The preacher must piece together the parts and announce their message. Is there a Father who loves us?

I do not wish to press a figure too far—it is always dangerous but it is interesting to note the fact that in an automobile factory there is specialization to an unusual degree. Nevertheless, the parts must come down an assembly line at last if there is to be an automobile. The scholarship of the minister must rest upon full understanding of, and respect for, specialization; but it must seek those syntheses that enable man to be sure where value lies, to be certain of where he wants to go, to be the possessor of proper direction as well as burning desire. It is not to discount scholarship to raise question concerning overspecialization. Anyone who is charged with the very difficult task of appointing ministers to churches knows that some of our "theological factories" have not paid sufficient attention to the assembly line and that some of its products lack steering wheel or brakes, some fail to install motors, and all too many forget ignition.

I like to think of the preacher as an "artificer in ideas," to borrow a lovely phrase from Lord Dunsany. Said he:

> Of all the materials for labor, dreams are the hardest, and the artificer in ideas is the chief of workers, who out of nothing will make a piece of work that may stop a child from crying or lead nations to higher things. For what is it to be a poet? [He might have said a preacher.] It is to see at a glance the glory of the world, to see beauty in all its forms and manifestations, to feel ugliness like a pain, to resent the wrongs of others as bitterly as one's own, to know mankind as others know single men, to know nature as botanists know a flower, to be thought a fool, to hear at moments the clear voice of God.

I am not discussing collectors of ideas. Ideas must be collected. Beetles must be collected; so, too, old china, worn-out furniture, Currier and Ives prints, stamps, autographs, recently manufactured antiques, geological specimens, and first editions. Have you visited the museumlike home? Collectors of ideas have their place. In the Kremlin are the relics of the ages, the gowns of the empresses, the carriages of kings and czars, glorious icons, and priestly robes. Someone collected this material, and wisely so. It possesses great value for future historians, and may give an occasional theme for a dissertation. But the city streets, the Kremlin offices, the rural lanes, are filled with men and women who are working with ideas rather than collecting them.

I am not discussing students of ideas. We must provide for students, certainly. Man cannot live without the men who ask, Whence? What? Whither? any more than he can live by bread alone. The research expert who can trace the long-time development of an idea, who can take us to the moment when the concept "the rights of man" was conceived, is a necessary figure. So too the scholar who can tell us what an idea means and whence an idea may take us is a constructive servant; although I am inclined to think that prediction in the matter of the working out of ideas is less valuable than scientific appraisement of the idea in action.

I am not discussing the "wearers of ideas," the debutante who purchases a string of ideas to wear at her coming-out party, the colors of the ideas dictated by the orchid dress and hung about her neck like pearls. If the young lady has ascertained the proper ideas to wear by a close perusal of that philosophical bluebook written by the well-known Emily Post, then, of course, all is well. If, on the other hand, she picked them up at some finishing school—mark well the word "finishing"—then God help her. I have religiously refrained from mentioning similar chains of pearls worn by elephantine matrons who, in discussing a philosopher, so often say, "I think he is gorgeous, don't you?"

No, for a moment I would stress the artificer in ideas. Is it too much, as far as the preacher is concerned, to say that ideas have meaning in so far as they can be applied? I do not mean that the activity involved in the application is the essential thing, not at all. Was James right when he said, "The ultimate test for us of what a truth means is indeed the conduct it dictates or inspires?" The artificer in ideas has been a collector and student of ideas but not a collector or student as such. Rather, his purpose is to build. Before he applies an idea to achieve an end, he insists that his generalizations shall report to the physician called reality and be thoroughly examined. That naked moment may be embarrassing for many a lovely idea; but the intellectual health of the community demands that the tests of science be applied

—that ideas, no matter how beautifully dressed, shall be examined, measured, weighed, pounded, fed bismuth, blood-pressured, sugar-tested, X-rayed. When an idea has passed the tests, the artificer in ideas, not forgetting the necessity of periodic examination to be sure the idea continues to measure up, seeks to use it, work with it, build something, put it into circulation.

I am pleading for a scholarship that will bring the preacher into an understanding of the experience of the race. Consequently, I would stress the place of literature and drama in his preparation. I am assuming that he will be trained in the scientific method. But he must know man. William Lyon Phelps, in his little volume *The Excitement of Teaching,* said:

> A treatise on chemistry published in 1904 is as useless as the almanac of that year, whereas Hamlet, published in 1604, and a play by Euripides, produced in 406 B.C. are as true [now] as they were for their own age and generation. . . . It is a curious thing that we call novels "works of fiction, when they are works of eternal truth."

It is this very lack of an understanding of man that makes so much preaching boresome. Some sermons are Saharalike in the vastness of concepts: but, because their concepts are so utterly unrelated to life, they are as dry as the desert is broad. Phelps refers to Browning's "The Statue and the Bust." Browning describes a "brilliant, accomplished, purposeless young aristocrat as a 'swordless sheath.' " Yes, and many a sermon is like a jeweled sheath, but a sheath without a sword.

Professor A. N. Whitehead, in his *The Aims of Education*

and Other Essays, gets at this question of scholarship from the standpoint of preaching. He asks:

> Pray, what is religious education? A religious education is an education which inculcates duty and reverence. Duty arises from our potential control over the course of events. Where attainable knowledge could have changed the issue, ignorance has the guilt of vice. And the foundation of reverence is this perception, that the present holds within itself the complete sum of existence, backwards and forwards, that whole amplitude of time, which is eternity.[4]

He is particularly stimulating when he writes of the rhythm of education. He speaks of three stages in intellectual progress: the stage of romance, the stage of precision, and the stage of generalization. In the first, the stage of romance, the student enters a new world. It is a door opened to rooms never before entered. The subject matter has the vividness of novelty. Too many remain in the period of romance. They would pass the wonder on to others but are incapable of doing so. It is essential that the full rhythm be followed. The second stage is that of precision. The student must not lose the wonder, but the "width of the relationship is subordinated to exactness of formulation." It is the stage of grammar, the grammar of langauge and the grammar of science. It is the period of analysis. But now we enter the last, the period of generalization.

> It is a return to romanticism, with the added advantage of classified ideas and relevant technique. It is the fruition which has been the goal of the precise training. It is the final success.[5]

[4] Whitehead, *The Aims of Education and Other Essays* (New York: The Macmillan Co.), p. 23.

[5] *Ibid,* p. 30.

Education, Whitehead contends, consists in a continual repetition of such cycles.

When I use the term "scholarship," I am thinking of the threefold rhythm. The mind should be aglow in the face of the beckoning, romantic quality of experience. But the preacher must do the hard, painstaking work, must pass through that stage of precision, of analysis, the understanding of restricted area, until at last he reaches those generalizations that will stand, which in their very nature may be the first stage of a new rhythm.

V

Old Dr. Hoose suggested sympathy. This is essential if the scholarship of the preacher is not to be an end in itself. There is a tendency to find complete satisfaction in learning unless it is ever subordinated by sympathy to the service of man. We live in a day when the percentage of cultured men increases. Desclos says:

> Culture consists of certain traits that carry over—the understanding quickened and deepened, a breadth of outlook, a catholicity of sympathies, a refinement of taste, an appreciation of beauty, a delicacy of feeling, a sense of measure, a modesty of judgment, the critical habit of mind, that habit that is the very soul of liberty, the unbiased approach to any problem and the undaunted pursuit of its solution in a true scientific spirit.

Unfortunately, the development of the cultured personality has a tendency to separate men of good taste from the man of no taste, to create barriers between the untutored and the man of scientific mind. I met a pastor some time ago who objected strenuously to serving in a certain parish. He stated that the people were laboring people, that they could not understand him. He insisted that his culture was beyond them, that he lived in a realm of philosophy which they could not enter. Perhaps it was unkind, but I did suggest to that brother that Jesus of Nazareth saw no such barrier.

It has been said that there is too much religion by proxy and not enough by proximity. Sympathy is indispensable.

Dr. Hoose spoke likewise of mannerisms, calling upon the preacher to avoid them. I need not speak in this group of holy tone, of unnaturalness, of carelessness in dress. Surely a preacher must know that, even though the leopard cannot change his spots, the preacher with Energine and energy can remove his. I heard the Mayor of Newton say that a little girl had said he was the best mayor in the land. He sought the reason, and learned it. She said, "Whenever he meets me, he tips his hat, just like he does to the ladies."

The "called messenger" of our Lord is the minister whose scholarship has led him to an understanding of the revolution into which he has been flung, into a recognition of the need of common faith and common purpose, and at last to the conviction that in love lies the power capable of reconciling the interests of the one and the many; whose sympathies have driven him from the security of the study to the service of human beings who struggle and suffer and die but also learn and love and live; who, freed from the mannerisms that separate a man from men, gives his all in the name of the One who said, "The Son of man came not to be ministered unto, but to minister." Such a preacher will be heard in a revolutionary hour. Such a one personifies the beautiful command of Jesus: "Let your light shine before men; that they may see your good works, and glorify your Father who is in heaven."

It is strange indeed that light as a symbol should stand in

such a significant place in religion. Particularly so when so many have insisted that religion is a term synonymous with superstition. Edwin Arnold sings of "The Light of Asia," and tells the story of the gentle Buddha in his song. The Apostle John writes of "the light of the world," and brings to mankind the story of the conquering Christ. The Gospels speak of the followers of Jesus as "children of light," and we learn that his "life was the light of men." Couple for a moment the command of Jesus, "Let your light so shine . . ." with the compelling challenge of John Masefield, "Adventure on! The next to lighten all men may be you." Think that it is our privilege to stand upon some high vantage ground and look down upon the entire North American continent, particularly that section which we know as our country. We are in the days before the coming of the white man. It is evening, and we note the lights upon the continent. They are but the campfires of the Indians. The years come and go; and now we behold the lights of the settlements that tell the miracle-like story of the pioneer. Decades pass, and we look upon the vast clusters of lights shining in the darkness—Boston, New York, Philadelphia, Chicago, St. Louis, Denver, San Francisco. It is like fairyland, and the lights tell the story of the building of the cities. In another decade new lights appear upon the shining continent—the flashing beacons that mark the airways of the nation and tell the story of the interpid fliers for whom the blackness of the night has no fear. The lights tell of courageous men bent upon far journeys, their ships roaring through the night, at first dependent upon the flashing, rotating, signaling beacons but now hearing the voices of direction and, with instruments responsive to law, moving with unerring accuracy to their predetermined destination.

I like to think of the preachers of today as pilots who have set out for a far country, resolved to reach the land of religious reality. We must fly by the flashing beacons that mark the way. As we take off and find ourselves at last aloft, watch for the lights. Better yet, if you are sufficiently sensitive, listen to the Voice. Here is Moses, a bright light flashing out the message, "In the beginning God"—"Thou shalt have no other gods before me"—"Honor thy father and thy mother"—"Thou shalt not steal." The centuries rush by at dizzy speed, until the light of another beacon breaks through the blackness. It is Isaiah singing of the Suffering Servant who will save his people from their sins. Then a beacon blazes with the light of the very sun—Jesus of Nazareth—"Thou shalt love the Lord thy God with all thy heart, and with all thy soul, and with all thy strength, and with all thy mind; and thy neighbor as thyself"—"Greater love hath no man than this, that a man lay down his life for his friends"—"The truth shall make you free"—"Blessed are the meek; for they shall inherit the earth"—"Lo, I am with you always." And a near-by light that marks the turn of your course from east to west, the light of the Apostle Paul—"Whatsoever things are true, whatsoever things are honest, whatsoever things are just, whatsoever things are pure, whatsoever things are lovely, whatsoever things are of good report; if there be any virtue, and if there be any praise, think on these things." And if in our flying we are guided by the lights and sensitive to the Voice, we will take direction from that scholar-saint of yesterday whose light blazes up from his *Confessions* and shines most brightly in his *City of God*—Augustine. High up in the mountains a soft light gleams—that of the cavalier-crusader Francis of Assisi, who revealed in his person the meekness and the love commanded by his Christ. The lights increase. We are blest by another beacon, the intellectual Wesley, whose intellect proved ineffective until the cold heart became strangely warmed and the world became his parish. "Let *your* light so shine." This we cannot do unless we "adventure on."

And if you do, "the next to lighten all men may be you."

CHAPTER V

THE PASTOR IN A REVOLUTIONARY AGE

I would not idealize the pastor. Nonetheless, it is the true pastor in whom the people behold the ideal. It is written, "In the beginning God created the heaven and the earth"; and out of the darkness of the creative hour a voice was heard: "Let there be light." When at last man walked the earth, he fell upon his knees to worship and to sing:

> The unwearied sun, from day to day,
> Does his Creator's power display,
> And publishes to every land
> The work of an almighty hand.

He bowed in reverence before the Almighty. Milleniums were to pass before he could bow in love and sing his Hymn to Joy. Man beheld the majesty of God when light shone upon the darkness. He experienced the love of God when the Word was made flesh and the only begotten of the Father dwelt among us, full of grace and truth. It was then he heard, "I am the light." Majesty retained its glory but took on meekness, and the Holy One was seen to be One of humility; the Creator became Father; justice and mercy were united, and power and love became one. Thus we sing:

Joyful, joyful, we adore Thee,
  God of glory, Lord of love;
Hearts unfold like flowers before Thee,
  Opening to the sun above.

Melt the clouds of sin and sadness,
  Drive the dark of doubt away;
Giver of immortal gladness,
  Fill us with the light of day! [1]

It is not unduly to exalt the pastor to stress the truth that ideals become meaningful for most men when beheld incarnate in other men. Millions may hear the voice of the preacher whose message moves from microphone to receiving set, and I would be the last to discount that great service; but the masses of men are more likely to be moved by a message revealed in a good man who dwells among them full of grace and truth.

By dwelling among them, I do not mean merely residing in the same city. One of the most brilliant of the younger preachers of the nation, whose full giving of self to his people belies his advice to theological students, was so eager to stress the necessity of hard and continuous study that he said, perhaps facetiously, "I never call unless the request is accompanied by a document certifying that the member has a temperature of 103.2." The Beatitudes take on new meaning, however, when the Teacher who said, "Blessed are they that mourn; for they shall be comforted," becomes a brother to Mary and Martha and makes inquiry concerning Lazarus.

[1] From *Poems of Henry van Dyke*. Copyright, 1911, by Charles Scribner's Sons.

It is recorded, "Jesus wept." And those near by said, "Behold how he loved him!"

A great preacher of a generation gone preached magnificently, and his thought lives in the lives of hundreds of students who crowded the church to hear him. He found pastoral care a burdensome duty and for him an almost impossible task. Thus he gave himself to the pulpit and the study. His was a church without an altar, a preaching place with center pulpit and platform chairs; and behind them were heavy curtains which the minister pulled apart when he entered the sancturay. An old lady who worshiped there once said, "When the curtains were opened and our minister preached, it was for me the voice of the Eternal. When the sermon was finished and the curtains hid him from us, we knew that he had gone to spend the week alone with God." I would be the last to call any man from hours with God, but I am a little fearful of the minister who spends no hours with man.

Phillips Brooks, whose preaching moved the hearts and minds of his generation and whose message was heard across the seas, is remembered and revered not alone because of magnificent hours in Trinity pulpit when the truth was preached, one might say torrentially, but also because of days given gladly to the poor and the rich, the weak and the strong, the untutored and the scholar. A great teacher of preachers told me that among his richest experiences was that of literally sitting at the feet of Phillips Brooks. It was the custom of the great preacher to invite a score of students to come to his home during the Lenten period and read the Bible together. It was all very informal, with its give and take of question and answer. A world-famous preacher, whose presence was sought by organizations of every sort, found time to sit with a handful of theological students—a pastor who gave life to the text, "The Son of man came not to be ministered unto, but to minister."

Eyes do not see and ears do not hear just because the preacher repeats the words of his Lord, "He that hath ears to hear, let him hear"—"He that hath eyes to see let him see." The preacher in a revolutionary age is much more likely to be heard and his ideas "seen" if he has been heard and seen in the homes of his people. The church has never developed a Crosley rating. I do not know how it could. But radio sponsors check up on the program, and the life of a commentator or a comedian depends upon his rating. The hearing of a preacher is related to his rating in his members' hearts. And that rating is determined more by the life in the parish than by the voice in the pulpit. I am speaking now of the thousands of parishes in city and country across the nation, recognizing full well that there are men who because of the sheer strength of their intellect, the clarity and winsomeness of their message, are heard and followed. Such men are priceless possessions of the Church, but their number is not legion.

The minister who has stood with a brokenhearted father and mother as together they watched a lovely child slip away, who has comforted them less by what he says than by what he is, and, in the last moment of committal, has read the lines with sorrow in his heart and triumph in his voice, is a man whom father and mother will hear with respect when he points the way to a better society and calls for the sacrifice such society may require.

It was but a year ago that my mother left us. It was her

wish that there be no eulogy, simply the reading of the beautiful service for the Burial of the Dead; and I knew that she wanted me to read the words that had brought comfort to unnumbered generations in their sorrow. I sat alone, thinking of the morrow and the service, of the yesterdays and a mother's love. The doorbell rang; and Willsie Martin, a friend of the years and pastor of the Wilshire Methodist Church of Los Angeles, was at the door. He called me Bromley; his voice was comforting. He did not speak of immortality, nor did he speak of sympathy. He was there; that was enough. There was a beautiful word about mother, a suggestion that he would arrange for the music, a smile, a handclasp; and he was gone. The little chapel of the Church of All Nations was filled with friends, the sunshine streamed through the stained-glass altar window and fell upon the flower-filled chancel, the service was read, and after a time we laid her beside my father in beautiful Inglewood. Associated forever with that sacred hour is a minister, a friend, a man. No words will ever fall from his lips that I will not listen to with respect. The pastor who has walked down dark valleys with his people and has shared, likewise, in their hours of great joy; the minister who has united youths in holy wedlock and has baptized their children; the friend who has shared in the successes of strong men and perhaps has given asked-for advice in their days of decision—such a man, when he speaks as a prophet, is heard, because he commands not only the eyes and ears of his people but their hearts as well. And all this he must do, knowing full well that in his own hour of sorrow or of triumph there is no pastor who will bear his burden or share his glory. He is to minister, not to be ministered unto. Perhaps it is because some ministers have never experienced the meaning of such ministration that they fail to recognize its vital nature.

A free pulpit rests on surer foundation when the preacher is loved by his people. A revolutionary age needs a free pulpit, and the wise preacher will seek to guarantee its freedom by the sympathy which true service brings forth. Upon more than one occasion a preacher whose congregation insists upon a change of minister has said, "Bishop, I do not understand it. Brother Smith at Calvary Church goes much further than I have in anything I have ever said, but his people do not demand a new minister." That is true, but Brother Smith has won the hearts of his people. There is no compromise in his message. There is comprehension in his membership. They know him. They trust him. They believe he preaches the Word of God as he in utter sincerity understands it. They examine their hearts when he speaks of sin. They know he has examined his own. That knowledge is born of the association with a good man who knows and serves his people, who is a *pastor*. The good shepherd is reputed to have known the names of his sheep. Some congregations think of their preacher as a hireling because the offering is too often the only personal relationship they have with him.

I

The pastor in a revolutionary age must respect man as man. Poor David Edstrom, sculptor of genius whose life was struggle filled with glory and despair, called me to his home one day. He wanted to talk about the publication of his autobiography. The home was a rented room on a plain street of Los Angleles. This man had known poverty, had lived in palaces. He had slaved as a stoker and dined with kings. He sought peace but never found it. "My misfortune," he wrote, "has been that my temperament and my art have not been necessities to the people of my time. There has been no real market for my essential talent." That was true. But the real tragedy of Edstrom's life is found in his own words of confession: "I am not a lover of my fellowman individually. Not my father nor my mother nor other relatives, friends, or comrades remain in my memory as being so desirable that I would care to see or live with them again. . . . I do not believe in the permanence of any personal relation."[2] I had read the typed sheets of that tragic story, and I remembered its closing line, "I am still traveling, and the years stretch out ahead full of mystery and adventure." The years were not many, and today Edstrom is but a memory among those who know art. Rupert Hughes wrote the Foreword to the autobiography. "Move over, Benvenuto Cellini," he commanded, "and make room on the narrow shelf of great autobiographies for this self-life of David Edstrom, a rival of your genius in sculpture, as in the revelation of himself and of the amazingly various people he has met." The volume is not read. You find it on the stands of secondhand bookstores, marked down now to fifty cents. Poor David Edstrom never knew that the joy he sought was never far away. It lay in love—love not of man as a generalization but of man individually. This he never learned. His adventure ended in a lonely room. It is not to criticize this remarkable man—I had profound respect for him—that I speak of his struggle and his sorrow. It is to say that no man can be a true pastor who does not love and respect human beings. He must have the

[2] *The Testament of Caliban* (New York: Funk & Wagnalls Co., 1937), p. 339.

song of Sandburg in his heart—"The people, yes, the people."

Phillips Brooks was right when he insisted that familiarity breeds contempt only in contemptible souls; nevertheless, the winning of culture seems to separate some souls from their untutored brothers. The great are humble and usually democratic, but the near great are less humble and affect the aristocrat. True culture, with its quickened understanding and catholic sympathy, is not divisive; but partial culture, with its pride in possession and pity for the unlearned, is. It is the pastor who learns there is more wisdom in a coalpit than is sometimes found in a faculty room. A mother who has reared a large family is often better qualified to discuss the love of God than the bachelor professor of systematic theology. A man who calls upon the people soon discovers that to take the profit motive out of the economic order is no guarantee that it will therefore leave the heart of man. He learns that true community is built upon love, which is the social bond, the cohesive factor, binding society in fellowship. Christianity is right and communism is wrong at this point. The communist knows that man is hungry. He appeals to the common hunger of men and calls upon them to be one that they may be fed. The Christian knows that man must love. He appeals to that universal need and calls upon men to love that they may be one, and the oneness of love makes bread for all—and brotherhood, too. If love fails, hunger determines. Where hunger rules, mad men fight for food. Where love rules, brothers make bread together. In one, the class united by hunger; in the other, the family united by love. It takes saints to commune. From the creedal intonation, "I believe in . . . the communion of the saints," to the practice of communion among brothers who seek to be saints is a long road. It is the pastor who knows how long!

Sin is not comprehended sufficiently when the lecture in systematic theology is ended. Its meaning becomes clearer when the pastor sits in a courtroom by a boy who has committed a crime and talks to the father, who had been too busy to be with his son until at last it is too late for the contribution of comradeship. The broken family may be a matter of statistical study and sociological observation in student days. But when a broken man comes with the sad story of his wife's desertion and requests that your own wife take his girls to the store to buy hats, because he doesn't know what girls need; when later you meet the wife and daughter of the man with whom his wife ran away, and you see the mother at a job and the daughter's dreams of education jeopardized—the broken home, and sin, are terms full of sorrow; and man's need of a new heart is an imperative. There is evil in the world, and evil acts express the evil intentions of men. We are children if we fail to see that evil men have deliberately chosen the ways of evil. Fascism is evil in its objective, evil in its methods; and fascism is fascist men in action, bent upon destroying the good; and the good lies in men who are good. This is not to be blind to social forces. It is to realize the need for conversion. The hearts must be changed. Sin has been with man from the days of the Garden, and I fear it will be present when man at last has made the world a "garden." It is not to be old-fashioned but to state the fact when we say the pastor's primary task is to save people from their sins. It is the pastor who learns the meaning of sin, who sees the struggle as it is. Like the pioneer who clears a living-place in the jungle, a man who would live righteously must fight, always fight, the encroachment of the jungle. It is there. It never admits defeat. The preacher must be a brother who helps his fellows keep the clearings in the soul and in society.

Yes, man sins and struggles. This the preacher must face. But man is sublime. This the preacher must know.

A letter I recently received abundantly illustrates man's sublimity in the face of trial. You cannot understand it unless you know certain facts. Fifteen years ago I received a telegram. It was from a poor preacher. His son was in the county jail in Los Angeles, charged with six counts of highway robbery—and he was guilty. He served in San Quentin. Finally, he was paroled to me. I had planned to see him through college, but he failed me. Subsequent crimes in New York resulted in a long sentence in Sing Sing and later in Dannemora. I have written to him through the years. A letter from him told of the death of his mother and an injury to his brother. I wrote a letter to the father. Here is a part of the father's reply:

DEAR BISHOP OXNAM:

Your good letter concerning the death of Mrs. ——— and the accident to ———, in which he lost both eyes, two fingers, and part of one foot, is at hand. I had not written of these things, for I have a feeling that circumstances have already made you a heavy bearer of my sorrow. Your good letter comes like the outreaching hand. I thought ——— [referring to the boy in prison] would kill me. Then Mrs. ——— went, after two operations for cancer, and now I am still struggling to save enough of ——— [his injured son] so he can get along. He has had four operations and will have another in June. Sorrows differ. Standing amid them, we see both God and humanity differently. They change our outlook on life and destiny. We enter into the "Far more exceeding might of glory." I now know God as I could not have known him —and so I believe I am more efficient. I have a six-point country circuit and preach to three different churches each Sunday. They have paid me $397 in the past six months. . . . I am in good health and happy in my work. God knows I am trying to be and do my best. . . . You mean more to me than you know. Blessings on you, dear man.

With great appreciation and love . . .

And I say, God bless him!

The pastor must respect man as man. He must see men in terms of their possibilities. He must see them as sons of God. His reading will help him to understand and to serve; but close association with a great surgeon, friendship with an inspiring teacher, visits in the home of a great executive who is also a father, fellowship with a leader of labor, hours with the boys and girls of the parish, will bring to him, as nothing else can, the goodness of human beings—their integrity, kindness, and love; their worth. More men have been brought to Christ by the preaching of his love than by the denunciation of their sin. And more men are held fast to their resolves by the pastor who has faith in the essential goodness of all men than by the brother who sees his fellows as degraded beings to be snatched from the burning. It is such faith that moves men from the defensive to the offensive. The pastor who conceives his pastoral work to be that of a counselor in the study finds himself dealing with problem situations and, if he is not careful, he begins to see all men as problems. True enough, all have fallen short of the glory of God. But there are many who fight the good fight and win the crown of glory.

When I held my first annual conferences and, as is the

practice of the Methodist Church, faced the responsibility of appointing the ministers to their churches, I, of course, had many interviews with preachers. I thought it would be informing to keep a record of what the preachers discussed, and this I did. I was amazed and disheartened to find that of the first two hundred who conferred with me, every one but one had talked about money. I began to misjudge my brothers. There was good reason for them to discuss money. Preachers are fathers, and their children are very precious to them. They have managed upon low incomes, and most preachers know their children are denied much. The time for college comes, and the salary is insufficient. I did not blame them, but it troubled me—preachers, all talking about money. Suddenly I realized that I was judging all of my brothers in the ministry by the ten per cent who had come to see me. Hundreds were carrying on, fighting it out without a word, somehow getting their children to college, some of them giving of their scanty means to help others less fortunate—wonderful people whose lives were changing communities. So, too, the pastor who does not see all his people. His view is limited. If he deals with those who have failed, or if he finds it congenial to be with the well-to-do, enjoying the dinners and the comforts, forgetting the poorer table, his understanding of his people is but partial, and, what is more important, his ability to preach as men must preach in a day of basic transition is limited.

It is the pastor who discovers the fallacies that lie in the so-called logic of much economic dogma. The late Robert Freeman let us see life through his understanding eyes when he told of a young man and a young woman who were walking up Orange Grove Avenue in Pasadena. They were in love and dreaming of the morrow. The young man looked upon the wide lawns leading to a mansion and whispered, "Sweetheart, I want to build a home like that for you. I want it now, now when we can enjoy it." It was not to become covetous that he desired wealth and such a habitation for that lovely girl. He did not know that as he spoke a woman, an invalid, looked from the windows of a great bedroom on the second floor and, seeing the girl with her beauty and her health, would gladly have given all just for the joy of walking up the avenue in the sunlight.

I drove through the mountains of Kentucky with William J. Hutchins when he was president of Berea College. He guided me to the cabins of the mountain folk, and we entered rude structures where for more than century children have been born, some to grow up in ignorance, some to die at an early age, an occasional individual to win great influence and power. One sensed an atmosphere of passion, of prejudice, of superstition; but he also found indomitable courage, rugged individualism, capacity to suffer. In one cabin we found a father, a mother, and eight children. The parents could not read nor write. The room was filthy, with no provisions for sanitation. One child was feebleminded. Tuberculosis was present. One boy suffering from tuberculosis had developed mastoiditis. Subsequently, a rupture occurred, and after months of suffering he died. From these hills the students come.

President Hutchins told me of one man who visited the mountain store and saw a bunch of bananas for the first time. The storekeeper said, "Try one."

The answer was abrupt: "No, I ain't goin' to."

"Why not?" asked the storekeeper.

The mountaineer replied, "I got so many tastes now I can't satisfy, I ain't goin' to add another one."

Hutchins went on to tell of a girl who possessed an innate yearning for the beautiful. She threw herself down in a furrow between the rows of corn, looked up to the stars, and prayed that she might go to Berea. She entered Berea and became an honor student. When the then owner of the *New York Times* and several distinguished political leaders visited Berea, they were so moved by the aspirations and abilities of these mountain youths that they decided to take ten of the best students on a tour of the East. This girl was chosen. She slept in a Pullman car for the first time in her life, visited the President of the United States, looked with wonder upon the bewildering achievement that is New York, heard Madame Homer sing, and returned to Kentucky.

These things the pastor must know if he would have a part in developing the common purpose which a common faith demands. I doubt that he will learn them if, after the proper morning in the study, he cannot bring himself to the exacting duties and privileges of the parish.

II

The pastor in a revolutionary age must never forget whose man he is, nor the One whom he represents.

When the Federal Bureau of Investigation was reorganized under Mr. J. Edgar Hoover's extraordinary leadership, the members of the criminal world took notice. They had no greater respect for the law, but they did develop a wholesome fear of its representatives. They called them Government men, which was soon shortened to "G-men"; and youngsters began to see the Dillingers as yellow and the Government men as heroic. The G-men won the respect of the nation, and the term will live. There is another body of G-men, not Government men but God's men. It is God they serve; it is his they are.

The preacher has been called a "man of God." He has been set apart, has knelt in sacred service and felt the ordaining hands of brother ministers placed upon his head while the bishop read, "The Lord pour upon thee the Holy Spirit for the Office and work of an Elder in the Church of God." He has worn robes or other garb of his calling. No one knows his shortcomings as truly as he himself knows them. God's man, this he is; and in the name of God he serves. His supreme loyalty is not to nation, to race, to class it is to God. In revolution, declaration of loyalty is demanded. The party cries are heard and the question asked, "Are you for us or against us?" The preacher must never forswear his God. No matter how crucial the hour, he is God's man, and God's alone. He must never abjure the moral law when acceptance of man-made law is commanded.

It is his Father's world. The earth is the Lord's, and the fullness thereof. The preacher who demands respect for personality must develop respect for the agencies upon which personality depends. God's man will realize that it is God's earth and that proper respect for God's sons involves respect for the soil upon which they depend. The metals and the oil, the forests and the rushing streams—the good earth and all its resources—are God's. The preacher who regards his calling as holy, the agent of the Holy One, must of necessity preach a doctrine of trusteeship that is revolutionary in nature. Current conceptions of property will be drastically revised. The preacher has something to say to the proprietor and to the proletarian. To do what one will with his own is to deny the fact of God's ownership. Trustees are not permitted to do this. Property is not to be held for power. It is to be held for use. The right to hold is to be determined by the use that is made, and the need of the community in the last analysis takes precedence over the right of the owner. God's man must make these matters clear, and they become clear when the pastor, the proprietor, and the proletarian consider the changes together in a fellowship whose final loyalty is to God rather than to class or to current theories of ownership or revolution. Thousands of such pastors could be the yeast that would leaven the lump.

The pastor must serve with full realization that he is practicing the presence of God. He belongs to the God of the universe, the God of immutable law, the God of the storm, the God whose handiwork is the heavens, the God who rouges the cheeks of a tiny flower and causes the birds to sing—God the Father, Almighty. How strange to find these words together, Father and Almighty; but there they are—the Father of all, the Creator of all. It is not that the pastor shall move among men with the suggestion that he bears the burdens of the universe, not that he shall cease to be intensely human, not that he shall be afraid to admit his limitations, but that he shall serve in the full knowledge of the God whose man he is.

The Archbishop of Canterbury has made this abundantly clear:

A vague theism is futile. The cutting edge of faith is due to its definiteness. The kind of deity established (if any is at all) by the various "proofs"—ontological, cosmological and the like—

is completely insufficient. The Christian has made a decision for God, who has spoken—in nature, in history, in prophets, in Christ.

It follows that the value of man and the meaning of history is to be found in the nature and character of God, who has thus made himself known. The value of a man is not what he is in and for himself—humanism; not what he is for society—fascism and communism; but what he is worth to God. This is the principle of Christian equality; the supreme importance of every man is that he is the brother for whom Christ died. This is compatible with many forms of social differentiation and subdivision. It is not compatible with any scheme which subjects a man's personality to another man or to any group of men, such as the government or administrators of the state.

The purpose of God is the governing reality of history. The nature of God is a righteousness which is perfect in love; his purpose, therefore, is the establishment of justice in all relationships of life—personal, social, economic, cultural, political, international. Many "humanists" share that aim, and Christians may well co-operate with them in practical policies from time to time. But a "decision for God" involves a sharp separation in thought, and, therefore, in the long run in practice, from many dominant tendencies of our time which seek the whole fulfillment of man's life in his earthly existence.

God has given to man freedom to decide for him or against him. This freedom is fundamental, for without it there could be only automatic obedience, not the obedience of freely offered loyalty. God always respects this freedom to the uttermost; therefore, freedom is fundamental to Christian civilization.

But though man is free to rebel against God, and can indeed do marvels through science and human wisdom in controlling his own destiny, yet he cannot escape the sovereignty of God. To deviate from the course of God's purpose is to incur disaster sooner or later—and sooner rather than later in so far as the deviation is great. The disaster ensues by "natural laws," as scientists use that phrase—that is, by the causal processes inherent in the natural order. But these laws are part of God's creation, and the disasters which they bring are his judgments.

Yet because man has so great a power to shape his own destiny, he is responsible for using this. Belief in God is used by many Christians as a means of escape from the hard challenge of life; they seek to evade the responsibility of decision by throwing it upon God, who has himself laid it upon them. Faith in God should be not a substitute for scientific study but a stimulus to it, for our intellectual facilities are God's gift to us.

As the first great commandment is that we love God with all our being, so the second is that we love our neighbor as ourselves. Here we are not concerned with that duty, but with the fact that underlies it whether we do our duty or not—not with what ought to be, but with what *is*. This is that we stand before God—that is, in ultimate reality—as bound to one another in a complete equality in his family. Personality is inherently social; only in social groupings can it mature, or indeed fully exist.

The pastor is God's man, and his labors are revolutionary in nature. They seek to bring men who in freedom have rebelled against the law of God to such obedience that God's will shall be done on earth, even as it is in heaven.

Such a pastor soon realizes that he has a stake in fields heretofore pre-empted by others. He must work with others to establish the conditions under which truth may be discovered. The truth frees, but antecedent to its freeing effect lies the necessity of maintaining the conditions under which truth may be found. He must co-operate with others in creating the techniques whereby truth may be applied; he must see that full publicity is given discovered truth and proposed techniques. He sees that truth frees but that it can enslave. The scientist may lay hold upon the truth—the laws that govern flight, for instance. That truth, applied, means the airplane, which can annihilate distance and help to make man one, or annihilate civilization and make man a beast. It is not necessary for man to climb the steeps of Sinai, to return with the tables of the law, nor to destroy the law when beholding the lawbreaker. It is necessary to bring all application of the law into harmony with the moral law itself. The application of truth for selfish ends violates the moral law.

The pastor has interest not only in preserving full liberty to worship, to preach, to teach for the Church but also in preserving the liberty which self-government demands for home and school. When the state seeks to determine the faith of the citizen, the Church becomes concerned. It refuses to admit the right of a political party to answer the question "What is man?" when such answer calls for acceptance. It will not accept the dictum of the state when the question "What is the nature of God?" is under discussion. In his *Church, Community* and *State* J. H. Oldham put its position with great force:

> The Christian Church is committed by its central affirmations to the belief that the life of man finds its meaning and fulfillment in a community of persons. God has spoken to us in his Son. He has revealed Himself through His word. The word—used in the widest sense to include every form of self-expression—is the means by which persons communicate with persons. In addressing us God invites from us a response. He asks for trust, loyalty and obedience. Through our response to the word addressed to us we become responsible persons and only through such response to the Father of our spirits can we become truly persons. God adopts us as sons and admits us to a life of communion and personal intercourse with Himself. His Word to us is a word which binds us to our fellow men and unites us with them in a community where love rules. God bids us serve Him as His free sons in the only way we can serve Him, by ministering

to the needs of our fellow men. What we do to them He accepts as done to Himself. The love of God and the love of our neighbour are inseparable. For Christians the worship and service of a personal God, whom we have learned to know as our Father, and relations of responsibility and love towards our fellow man—relations which can exist only between persons—are the supreme and ultimate things. The Church is the community of those who have been redeemed from a self-centered existence which is death into the objectivity and freedom of a life of personal response to the demands of persons, a life of trust and loyalty, of faith and love.

The reason for emphasizing this central element in Christianity is that it is precisely this understanding of the life of man that is denied by all the doctrines that are in the ascendant today. It is denied by those who maintain that the final and decisive thing in life is the blood or race. Man on this view derives his being from below, from some blind, irrational power, and not from the word of the living God, which comes to him from above. The priority and supremacy of the personal is rejected by those who contend that man's ultimate loyalty is owed to a nation or a state. It is repudiated by those who hold that man's primary need is bread and that his life is wholy determined by material realities. The Christian doctrine that persons can be persons only in community is equally opposed to the view which regards man as an individual existing in his own right, concerned primarily to develop his own "personality," free to pursue his self-centered aims, unfettered by bonds which unite him inseparably with his fellow men. Against this self-seeking individualism the modern collectivist systems are a justifiable reaction. But, notwithstanding the profound differences between them, they all have their origin in the same secular mind from which individualism sprang and in the same mistaken confidence in the self-sufficiency of man, and consequently they are in danger of setting up forms of collectivism which, as much as the individualism they replace, are a denial of the true nature and meaning of community, which is love and trust between persons, in fellowship and mutual service.[3]

[3] Harper & Bros., 1935, pp. 36-37.

As God's man, the pastor must create within the parish the spirit capable of unending struggle, no matter what the cost, against those views that would give ultimate loyalty to a person, a party, a program, rather than to God. But he must keep his head and let men see that building a new world is a bigger job than some imagine—some little men who would take God's place and make all things new.

The Czechoslovakian playwrights Karel and Josef Capek in biting satire have dealt with the problem of creating a new world in the play *Adam the Creator*. Adam, like many a man before him—he was not the first Adam—has soured on the world. He is out not to save it but destroy it. He has invented the Cannon of Negation which, when fired, will negate everything. The hour comes, the cannon is fired, and nothing remains but barren earth and a hopelessly desolate horizon. There is nothing but Adam. In denying all else, he had forgotten to deny himself. Empty nothingness. There is no one to praise his destruction.

Then comes the voice of God: "Adam, why have you done this?"

Adam answers, "Because the world was badly and unjustly made. For instance—"

Before he can finish, the voice thunders, "Create it anew yourself."

"But how? And what from?"

The voice continues, "It is terrible to create. Rise, . . . Adam, create!"

And Adam soon realizes that it is easy to *say* create a new world. But how is one to do it? To think of something new, something better, that's the rub.

At last he resolves he will create a superman, one to surpass what was; but suddenly he queries, "But why the devil must it be a man? I can be man." He will create a superwoman. He kneels to fashion the clay.

> I will create. In passion of creating
> I plunge ecstatic hands into the clay.
> The miracle of life itself, behold,
> Is forming in the clay; no slave of sex,
> No woman, but a goddess. You shall not
> Be under man's dominion, but shall be
> Mistress of your own lot; not given to man
> As prey but to be reverenced by him.

The clay is moulded. He rises and cries:

> Goddess, awake! Rise, new and finer woman!
> You'd never think creating's such hard work.
> Come, don't lie like a statue!—Not a movement.
> Ah, I've not given her the breath of life.

He breathes upon the clay and commands:

> Eve, thou who'rt beauty, strength, and woman, thou
> Miracle most divine, see, the creator
> Has kissed thy forehead with the breath of life.
> Live!

Eve raises herself, and Adam in rapture exclaims, "It's come to life! Then I do know how to do it. Eve, are you really alive?"

And Eve, getting up in cool interrogation asks, "Who calls me?"

Adam answers, "I, your creator. I salute you upon my knees, divine creation!"

And Adam, who has created the goddess, the superwoman, a being not under man's dominion, hears her answer: "Stay on your knees." [4]

Men who would create the morrow must learn that they must live in the tomorrow they create. The revolutionary creator must live with his progeny, and it is well for him to remember that "brathood" is not brotherhood.

III

The pastor in a revolutionary age must be worthy of the respect of his people, intellectually, morally, spiritually. The faith he preaches must be the faith he lives by. He knows how difficult this is, because a man, no matter how spiritual, lives in and is forced to accommodate himself to his day. The Apostle Paul lived in a day of slavery; and, even though he saw something more in Onesimus the runaway slave, the beloved brother of his vision returned to Philemon, the master. A contemporary saint must live in a competitive society. It is almost impossible for a man to be in the world and not of the world. Nonetheless, the pastor moves in and out among the homes of his parish, pledged to the Christian way, the Christian truth, and the Christian life. In the spirit of Christ, he is called upon to reprove, to demand reform, and, better than either, by his example to renew the command of his Lord, "Follow me." He dare not administer the Holy Communion if any brother hath aught against him. If the service await this test, much calling, much searching of heart, much forgiveness, must precede it. He is one who has grounded his conception of right in theology; the rights of a man rest in the fact that he is a son of God. These he

[4] New York: Richard R. Smith, 1930, pp. 16, 17, 20, 21, 22.

cannot deny to himself; they are written upon the tablets of the universe. Such rights are linked with responsibility; they inhere in the same plan and must be linked in thought by a hyphen—right-responsibility—a kind of cosmic *noblesse oblige,* the obligations of sonship that, observed, mean nobility.

The pastor will make this clearer by his conduct than by his labored expositions. Haushofer, the geopolitician, in his discussion of the geopolitics of the Pacific, argued that power and purpose must be kept in balance, and concluded that Japan was doomed because her purpose had become greater than her power. The Christian is not confronted with the question of power. It is a matter of purpose. He is promised all power; but the available power is seldom used, because the Christian fails to keep his purpose in balance with the power. This is quite easy to set down in a few lines; it is most difficult to keep this balance throughout a single life.

Is the pastor able when his own son dies to reveal in his person the faith in immortality he proclaims? I stood beside Dan Poling on a certain occasion. I knew that his chaplain son had gone down at sea. I knew that this strong son and other chaplains on that ship had given their life preservers to others. I knew that they stood at their posts and read a prayer as the ship settled into the sea. He was the same Dan Poling as before this great loss, strong of body, keen of mind. He spoke in the same voice. I thought I detected a new light in his eyes; perhaps I imagined it. He was speaking before the Executive Committee meeting of the Federal Council of the Churches of Christ in America, pleading for chaplains to serve our men who serve us. I had written him a letter immediately upon receiving the tragic news, and he had replied:

MY DEAR BROMLEY OXNAM:

Returning from ten weeks overseas, I find your letter of April 5. It was a very wonderful letter my friend, and one that we shall always cherish.

We have now word from the War Department that after completing their investigation, they must list our son Clark as having lost his life in action on February 3 in the North Atlantic area. But he remains where we placed him before he was born—in God's will.

Significant of his life and high faith are these words from his last letter to me: "It now appears that I am going into a 'blind alley,' but if, when I get there, I find one other man, then there will be three of us."

I just missed your son in Algiers. He came through while I was at the front in Tunisia. I was so sorry not to see him.

With love to you,

Sincerely,

DAN

Can I repeat with honesty "Nothing can separate me from the love of Christ"? Dan Poling could say that!

If the minister preaches brotherhood, do the people in the parish see conduct revelatory of such an attitude as Dr. Frank P. Graham, a Southerner, expressed in a recent decision of the War Labor Board on the question of equal pay for Negro and white workers? Wrote President Graham: "Slavery gave the Negro his Christianity. Christianity must give the Negro his freedom. This freedom must give the Negro equal rights to home and health, education and citizenship, and an equal opportunity to work and fight for our common country."

In his essay on Goethe, Emerson speaks of a property possessed by Goethe, "an habitual reference to interior truth." Subsequently, he uses such phrases as "a certain probity," "a controlling sincerity," and tells us Goethe "taught men how to dispose of . . . mountains miscellany, and make it subservient." Some pastors are so mastered by the "mountainous miscellany" of the parish routine that they give the impression of a heavily burdened pack animal whose nature is subservience. Not only does the parson's car that becomes the parish bus compete with the company chartered busses but, as a bus driver, the pastor has little time to impress his people with those characteristics of probity, sincerity, and habitual reference to interior truth upon which travel to a better land is really dependent. In all that I suggest concerning the pastor I am assuming that he brings the mountainous miscellany under subservience. This he must do if, as preacher, he maintains the study life that is essential to hold the respect of his hearers.

When T. R. Glover, whose *Jesus of History* has been read in many lands, addressed the Los Angeles City Club, he was asked, "What is your opinion of Mr. Ford's statement that history is the bunk?"

He replied, "I dare say all the history he knows is the bunk."

The opinions of a great manufacturer are given wide hearing, but the opinions of an obscure preacher will have no hearing at all unless they reveal the study he commends to his people.

Flight Lieutenant James Sinclair, sometime Rhodes scholar, is reported in *Time* to have made a devastating speech in the House of Commons at Ottawa when home on leave. Speaking for the soldier, he said:

> The Seaforth private will go back to civilian life with $45 while the major general will get $600. This is a case of: To them that have had, more shall be given, and to them that have had very little, very little shall be given. . . . [The men overseas] know the bitter disillusionment of soldiers in the last war. . . . They know the hungry 30's. They are determined this is not going to happen to them. . . . I tell this house if these men return to such conditions, their song will not be "Land of Hope and Glory"; it may be the "Red Flag." [5]

Such men will fill our pews tomorrow if they return to a pastor who serves them, endures hardship, and faces danger as their chaplain did; but such men will demand a gospel that stands critical scrutiny. They have acted upon their orders. They will demand action in the realm of religion, or they will desert. Santayana once wrote, "The world is full of conscript minds, only they are in different armies, and nobody is fighting to be free, but each to make his own conscription universal." Preaching that gives such an impression in a revolutionary age will fail to hold the allegiance of men who have come to see that freedom really matters.

Reason is a requisite of revolution. The pastor must be a reasonable person, free from domineering dogmatism but loyal to the certainties of his faith, maintaining his convictions in conduct, but co-operative in spirit, honest in his search for reality, purged of superstition. If his theories will not explain the facts, he must be ready to restudy his theories. Max Thorek in *A Surgeon's World* records:

[5] *Time*, Feb. 21, 1944, p. 23.

I was present once when Professor Richard Jaffe, master pathologist, was about to expound the findings of the autopsy he had just completed on a young man who had died from an unknown cause. Every organ and every tissue was carefully scrutinized by the great doctor. The silence was almost audible as the doctor's frown grew and grew. Slowly he reposited the well examined organs in their proper abode. He began to speak, not to us, his audience, but to the corpse. "Come, come, now, young man," he said. "You have no bizness here. . . . From zis investigation, we must truly conclude you are shamming us as dead and are able to walk. For truly . . . well . . . zere is nossing ronk wiz you!" And he kept on frowning while the amphitheatre rocked with laughter. I almost thought I saw a derisive grin on the corpse's face.[6]

It is not easy to speak with the restraint of the scientist when essaying to speak for the Almighty. There is danger that the preface "Thus saith the Lord" may be followed by much that should have been introduced by "Thus saith the preacher."

When my son was a little fellow, he evidenced a bit of positiveness that stood him in good stead when he was a chaplain on the Anzio beachhead, embarrassing as it was then. We were on a streetcar. A lady suffering from a nervous affliction which kept her head turning from right to left as though she were saying "No" sat down across the aisle. Philip, a friendy child, spoke up and asked a question that should have been answered in the affirmative. The poor woman shook her head. He was puzzled, and he disagreed, calling out, "Is, too!" The woman shook her head, and he, with his integrity at stake, shouted, "Is, too!" With the car in hysterics, we finally managed to quiet the debative young-

[6] Philadelphia: J. B. Lippincott Co., 1943.

ster, who no doubt continued to whisper to himself, "Is, too."

It will do no good to answer the head-shaking negatives with argumentative "Is, too's." The pastor must know why heads shake and when to announce his affirmations. If his mind is open, he may learn that radicals become reactionary and reactionaries may be forward-looking. It is said that E. W. Scripps, who founded the Scripps-Howard chain of papers, spent much time upon a far Western ranch. When queried on the subject, he remarked: "I'm a rich man, and that's dangerous, you know. But it isn't the money that's the risk, it's the living around other rich men. They get to thinking all alike; and their money not only talks, their money does their thinking, too. I come off here on these wide acres of high miles to get away from my sort. . . . So I don't think like a rich man. They talk about the owner of newspapers holding back their editors." He laughed. "It's the other way with me. I get my boys, bright boys, from the classes that read my papers; I give them the editorship and the management, with a part interest in the property; but as soon as the profits begin to come in, say in a year or so, they become conservative and I have to boot them back into their class, and even then. . . . Corruption? Yes, but it's they that corrupt me and my papers, those bright boys from the streets."

In his Lyman-Beecher Lectures years ago Phillips Brooks said, "Preaching is the communication of truth by man to men." Yes, but how can the truth be communicated unless the man knows men? R. W. Dale, in *Nine Lectures on Preaching,* expressed the thought thus: "When men leave the university they are apt to suppose that the same laws which should govern the search for truth have authority in the propagation of it." It is the pastor who comes to know men, and such a man becomes the medium through which the truth can be communicated. He knows that preaching can never be the calm, dispassionate, and objective discussion of the classroom. It is a presentation of fact, certainly, but it is also an expression of personal conviction. A man's life is at stake when the lawyer pleads. So, too, when a man preaches.

The pastor who has come to know his people preaches with the assurance that he need now but convince their minds; he has already won their hearts. His people become one in their love for him; and, if his preaching be worthy, they move as one in the name of one Lord. Christianity is the religion for a revolution that would exalt the person, because at its center stands the Person exalted. It is the pastor who makes religion personal. It is he who can lead his people to the Person divine.

CHAPTER VI

THE REVOLUTIONARY CHRIST

My first reaction was one of revulsion! The painter's brush had become party to blasphemy. Orozco had gone too far. Had he not made caricature of the Christ and brought contempt upon the Cross? Strangely enough, the painting possessed sufficient magnetic attraction to hold me fast; suddenly its meaning gripped me, and my mood became one of repentance. I speak again of the overpowering murals in the Baker Library at Dartmouth College and of the work of Orozco, the artist of revolutionary revelation.

It is the last panel, done in rich colors—the deep browns of the soil, the deeper reds of blood. A towering figure of Christ dominates all. He stands with feet apart, flesh torn, triumphant. At his side is an ax, the handle grasped tightly by his right hand. In the background are temples and tabernacles overturned in ruins amid the spoils of war, as though some terrible earthquake had made scorn of the religions of man. Rising above shattered stone and splintered timber is the Christ. Then one sees that the ax has been laid to the root of the tree. The cross itself has been cut down. It lies beside the stump from which it has been severed, and the Christ stands astride it.

Had the artist sought to ridicule the Cross? I thought. Was

this sacred symbol of my faith to be made the sport of a revolutionist?

And then I knew that a dead figure hanging from a cross is not the sign of my faith. True, there could have been no Christian faith without the cross; but death upon the cross and that alone would not have summoned deserters, who had been disciples, to crusade and to crosses of their own. The cross, as well as death, was swallowed up in victory. Our Lord is not a poor broken figure hanging from the tree—hands imprisoned by cruel nails and feet held fast by spikes, eyes that do not see and ears that do not hear, a tongue that is stilled, a body with spirit gone—whose message is Miserere. No, he is Christ triumphant, living now and forever more, freed from the flesh, victor over men who vainly believe they can destroy the spirit by crucifying the body. He lives; and, lest the misguided with creedal crown and nails of fanaticism would make him prisoner to the cross, he lays the ax to the cross itself. It falls; and the sorry inscription, "This is the King of the Jews," is crushed beneath the cedar. He is King of kings and Lord of lords. He lives; his eyes do see, beholding in every man a brother and envisioning what man may become as a son of God; his ears do hear the cries of the oppressed, the low moan of the sorrowful, the glad shouts of children at play, and, like the sound of the sea, the swelling notes of joy chanted by the millions of men in that morrow when justice shall roll down as a mighty stream and righteousness shall cover the earth; his hands and feet are free, the hands of healing, the feet of the second mile; he speaks, and men learn of the way and the truth and hear that judgment will be rendered upon the simple rule, "Inasmuch as ye have done it unto one of the least of these my brethren, ye have done it unto me"—"Enter thou into the joy of thy lord."

Did the artist seek to speak as Paul spoke, to affirm that the last enemy, death, is destroyed, that all things are subdued to Christ? I do not know. Perhaps it was less a matter of theology than of social proclamation. Christ, alive and free from an imprisoning cross before which many bow to worship but from which too few hear the summons "Follow me"—how can he march, if he be nailed to a cross?—a living Christ, who, having been lifted up, does draw all men because of his gift of self but who leads all men because of his mastery of death—this is the revolutionary Christ, whose message will be Jubilate!

I

The essence of Christ's revolutionary impact lies in three simple words: principle, practice, pattern. Here the truth precedes the way, and truth and way reveal the life.

He proclaimed the principle of self-realization.

He called for the practice that would enthrone the principle in individual and social life.

He revealed in his Person the pattern. The Word was flesh and dwelt among us. The revolutionary Christ! It was he who said, "Follow me." And even then he added, "And lo, I am with you always." It is Weymouth who puts it, "And remember, I am with you always, day by day."

G. A. Studdert-Kennedy understood the principle of self-realization enunciated by Jesus. He took a term of reproach and hallowed it when he wrote "He Was a Gambler Too."

> And, sitting down, they watched Him there,
> The soldiers did;

There, while they played with dice,
He made His Sacrifice,
And died upon the Cross to rid
God's world of sin.
He was a gambler too, my Christ,
He took His life and threw
It for a world redeemed.
And ere His agony was done,
Before the westering sun went down,
Crowning that day with its crimson crown,
He knew that He had won.[1]

This is the revolutionary principle. Man must take his life and throw it for a world redeemed, must "bet his life there is a God" (as Donald Hankey wrote in the last war and as some have found in this bitter hour), must become the very incarnation of gambling by risking all on the moral law and the love of God. He is done with the question of physical survival. He lives as he gives; and if he gives all, he gives for all, and forever. This is the call to the talented. The greater the talent, the greater the responsibility to give; and giving lies in the service that makes all richer and none poorer. Here is the universal obligation to work. The principle Christ proclaimed was simple but sublime: *The self is realized in the complete gift of self for others.*

I know that the term "revolutionary" is objectionable. It is associated with contemporary doctrines in which violence is made virtue. It calls forth terrible memories, the gruesome guillotine and the bloodstained barricades. We cannot separate it from the brutal scenes of Odessa and St. Petersburg: in the former, the soldiers of the Czar in unbroken

[1] From *The Unutterable Beauty,* by G. A. Studdert-Kennedy (New York: Harper & Bros., 1930), p. 117.

phalanx pushing the people at bayonet point down the steps and into the sea; in the latter, the dead and the dying in the Square before the Winter Palace after their peaceful petitions had been ripped to shreds by the bullets of the poorly advised and fearful ruler, whose heart was cold. Nor can we forget the scenes so soon to follow—scenes of blood and battle in which brother killed brother, White slew Red, and Red slew White. Revolution speaks of terror, and releases the forces of the night. It was fitting that Mussolini's brutal legions should have worn black shirts; they were the powers of darkness. It was proper, too, that the storm troopers of Hitler should have been clad in brown! Like Cain, they were of the soil, their hands full of blood, and upon their lips the question that is always confession, "Am I my brother's keeper?" They were the troopers of the storm. And when the storm had passed, homes had become concentration camps, the liberty of the many had become the tyranny of the few. It is not to be wondered that "revolutionary" is an offensive term. But there is no other word that will do. Jesus did teach a principle of conduct that can only be described as revolutionary: self-realization by self-giving that may involve self-denial.

It is a revolutionary principle. Like the tocsin bell, it announces doom if denied; but, like the Angelus call, it promises peace if practiced. It is a gift of self that is expressed in love of brother and of God. Jesus came by the principle rightfully. His mother was a handmaiden of low estate, the first of low degree whom he exalted. I do not forget that she was of royal lineage, that in her veins flowed the blood of kings; but she was a peasant whose heart carried the aspirations of her downtrodden people. The generations have called her blessed; and when at last her Son is Lord of lords and King of kings, and the proud are scattered and the mighty put down, she will be magnified even as she magnified the Lord, for he will have showed the strength of his arm. The Magnificat was a song of revolution, sung by a maid of Nazareth who had found favor with God, whose Son should be called Jesus. Had not the angel whispered: "He shall be great, and shall be called the Son of the Highest. . . . And he shall reign . . . and of his kingdom there shall be no end"? What manner of king is this, a king upon whom rests the spirit of the Lord? He is a King who would make all things new—a King who proclaims the acceptable year of the Lord, preaches the gospel to the poor, heals the brokenhearted, brings deliverance to the captives and recovery of sight to the blind, and sets at liberty them that are bruised. This is a revolutionary conception of kingship, revelatory of the principle upon which self-realization depends. The reading of the lesson in the Nazareth synagogue became an act of revolution. His words were gracious; eyes were fastened upon him; but they knew he was the carpenter's son. And when the unaccepted prophet spoke of fufillment, the synagogue was filled with wrath; and they rose up and thrust him out of the city.

The revolutionary nature of the principle was grasped by the Apostle Paul, a Roman and a Jew, a man of pride and of very great strength, who made it abundantly clear to Corinthians whose conduct left much to be desired.

I may speak with the tongues of men and of angels, but if I have no love, I am a noisy gong or a clanging cymbal; I may prophesy, fathom all mysteries and secret lore, I may have such absolute faith that I can move hills from their place, but if I have no

> love, I count for nothing; I may distribute all I possess in charity, I may give up my body to be burnt, but if I have no love, I make nothing of it.[2]

When pride becomes beneficent, the proud count for nothing. The martyr whose dogmatism or hatred earned the gibbet makes nothing of it. This is revolutionary; surely the endowment given in pride counts for something. How can the widow's mite given in love count for more? Oh, the gift may count for much; but the giver makes nothing of it. Nor does the faith that can move mountains amount to anything unless the faithful possesses love. Preaching itself, the ability to prophesy and fathom mysteries and secret lore, even to speak with the tongues of angels, is but noisy gong or clanging cymbal without love. Paul had learned the secret of self-realization. He calls it the "secret for all sorts and conditions of life." And thus though he himself declared,

> I have been often at the point of death; five times have I had forty lashes (all but one) from the Jews, three times I have been beaten by the Romans, once pelted with stones, three times shipwrecked, adrift at sea for a whole night and day; I have been often on my travels, I have been in danger from rivers and robbers, in danger from Jews and Gentiles, through dangers of town and of desert, through dangers on the sea, through dangers among false brothers—through labour and hardship, through many a sleepless night, through hunger and thirst, starving many a time, cold and ill-clad, and all the rest of it,[3]

he could still say, "Wherever I go, thank God, he makes my life a constant pageant of triumph in Christ." This man may

[2] I Cor. 13:1-3, according to Moffatt, *The Bible, A New Translation* (New York: Harper & Bros., 1935).
[3] II Cor. 11:23-28, *ibid.*

have seen the pageants of triumph with which Rome honored triumphant generals. This was no Roman triumph. It was a revolutionary pageant, a pageant of triumph in Christ, in which the Triumphator bore in his body the marks of the Lord Jesus Christ, the scars that speak of the self realized in the gift of self for others.

Is the principle but another expression of perfectionist ethics? Is it realizable only among the few who separate themselves from the world? If the grace of God cannot effect such change of heart that the converted earnestly strive to be made perfect in love in this life, then our preaching is vain. The principle is written into the nature of things, and the self is realized when the principle is obeyed. There was but one Perfect Man, and obedience to the law meant death upon the Cross. The principle is less perfectionist when seen as social. True enough, society does not love, cannot give itself for others; nations cannot love other nations. It is the individual who loves. Nevertheless, when the individual in co-operation with other individuals establishes institutions based upon the principle that the service of each for all calls for the full spending of talent for others, the environment evokes the service that is expressive of love and the principle appears more practical and less perfectionist.

Bishop W. Y. Chen suggests that our difficulty in the preaching of love has been the stress on love as emotion rather than love as will. He once used a homely illustration:

> When I came to the United States to study, I found it difficult to eat your food. Slowly, I learned to do so. But there was one item in your diet that was impossible. It was cheese. Now the Chinese have no such product. To a Chinese, cheese-eating is like

soap-eating to you. So I refused to eat cheese. But I said to myself, "Cheese is here. It is a food. I must eat it." I could not. Finally, I said, "This calls for an act of will. I will not allow my distaste for cheese to determine my conduct toward cheese." So I ate cheese and I kept willing and eating until at last when I reached Germany for further study I could face the cheese that was on every table with a fair degree of friendship and, believe me, the day came when I could eat even Limburger cheese.

Bishop Chen was dealing with racial distaste, which is as real as his aversion to cheese, but which is overcome by love that is will.

II

Jesus was revolutionary because he demanded practice expressive of the principle. I cannot believe that the sacred words "This do in remembrance of me" referred alone to the distribution of the symbols of Holy Communion. If the washing of the disciples' feet was to reveal the greatness that lies in service, surely the bread and the wine were a call for volunteers brave enough and good enough to offer body and blood for the emancipation of man. What a commentary upon the Christian community is contained in the conclusion of the talented and consecrated leaders who drafted the Report of the American Section of the Commission on Intercommunion. They said: "Our studies . . . make it evident that both Intercommunion and full reciprocal open Communion are at present unattainable, even within the bounds of the Ecumenical Movement." Christians unable to kneel together at the table of the Lord! Recently, in Boston, Catholics, Jews and Protestants sat at one table. It was a banquet table, not a communion table. The customary tributes of such occasions were made, and we stressed our essential unity. Unfortunately, it was our fear, not our faith, that brought us together. The fascist threat lurked in the background of our thinking. But does our faith unite us? Yes, when the essence of our faith lies in the command of the Upper Room, "A new commandment I give unto you, that ye love one another." No, when the essentials are conceived in rubric and ritual, sacrament and Articles of Religion. Does the reference of the Lord to the fact that gifts must not be brought to altars if brothers have anything against us apply to the Eucharist? If my brother has aught against my theological views, my rigidly held practices of exclusion, should I turn from the symbols and become right with him? How incredible that a simple supper of an Upper Room should have become the occasion of century-long debate, tenaciously held but contradictory practice—a barrier, not a bond. With totalitarian tyranny knocking at the gates, Christians are unable to erect an altar before which all may kneel and become one in Christ Jesus. Does any serious man really believe that world law and order depend upon the theories associated with the administration of the Sacrament? Is economic justice to be won by revising the ritual? Is racial brotherhood to come by way of a Communion administered solely by men who are "properly" ordained? Is not the road to unity along the highway of service to our fellows and in the complete gift of self to others, so that at last we respect one another through the spirit and significance of the service rendered, recognizing finally that exhausting discussion of the Eucharist is less important than the breaking of our bodies and the shedding of our own blood in the interest of others? Jesus does demand the practice of the principle, and the practice awaits resolute love.

That conduct must be a derivative of love and not of self-interest is a revolutionary doctrine. Revolution commands action upon the basis of the principles of the revolution. The Christian confronts a serious problem here because his revolutionary leader demands so much. Jesus knew men were sinners. He knew that men who had left their nets and followed him were also men who might desert and deny him. Selfishness submits to love only after struggle. The denier was asked, "Lovest thou me?" He was ordered, "Feed my sheep." There was much of love and more of physical courage in this man when he stood in Gethsemane. There was less courage when in the Courtyard. But there came a day when he was a rock that could not be moved, and upon it the Church was built. Paul was transformed upon the Damascus Road; but the road to perfection was marked by the struggle to bring under subjection the instinctive drives of the body, the insistent summons to self-preservation, the innate self-assertiveness to which man is disposed. Paul could not tolerate indecisiveness that bordered on cowardice, and thus would have no more of John Mark. His letters were full of references to those who criticized him; his answers were at times stern, often devastating; and his recommendations were rigorous. He knew his weakness but believed there was strength sufficient, and therefore wrote his comrades, "My strength is made perfect in weakness." Nevertheless, there it is, the weakness and sinfulness of man in the face of strength and sinlessness of Christ. The preacher will do well to ponder the question, How can men conduct themselves according to the dictates of love and live in a society whose major decisions are determined by the dictates of self-interest?

The revolutionary principle is bound to the obligation to practice, and this means change that is revolution. The Christian way is not the way of violence; it is the way of love. But love must know. It is the love grown rich in knowledge that eventuates in a sense of what is vital. The practices must be of such a nature as to release the creative energies, keep man on the march that, please God, will never end, maintain and extend the research that brings new knowledge and the consequent release of man from the limitations of the physical. Who can envision the morrow that research and applied science will make possible! A man will be able to see and to speak to any brother anywhere in the world. New materials and abounding energy are literally pouring from the test tubes. The advocates of the self-interest philosophy argue that men have driven themselves into the dense undergrowth of the unknown and have scaled the peaks of mystery in order to satisfy some inner compulsion, and this desire to satisfy is self-interest. Some seek answers and some seek wealth, they say. But there is a difference! The true scientist seeks the truth, knowing that truth makes us free. The artist rises before the dawn that his canvas may record the clear light of morning, knowing that his work makes man richer. The engineer rears vast structures, tunnels the mountains, dams the rushing streams, controls the floods; and his fellow workers cause the deserts to bloom. The organizing genius brings man and machine and material together, and new wealth is created. And all of this, like the necessary toil of the men on the section gang, the skilled miners of the coal pits, the teacher in the classroom, the mother in the home, contributes to the common life. Here is necessary service; and if social approbation is won and the worker lives in the esteem of his fellows, no doubt the self is glad and legitimate self-interest satisfied. These activities differ from those predatory practices through which the natural resources of a nation are seized by the strong, and the creative workers for all time to come are required to pay tribute to an owning group simply because it owns. When the getter is glorified and the giver is pauperized, it is but natural that men should seek glory by way of getting; but when giving is exalted, is it not likely that men who would be exalted will turn to giving? Harmony is more likely in a giving than in a getting economy.

The inadequacy of the competitive economy is seen in the fact that its chief advocates strive to eliminate its central feature, namely, competition. This is but an expression of the self-interest by which the economy is driven. The self-interest economy is self-destructive. The progress that competition was supposed to develop is retarded by the fact that self-interest sees in monopoly a method of greater immediate return. Thus the troublesome competitor is eliminated, prices are fixed, the consumer is exploited, and the men who control the monopoly are enriched. Scarcity is seen as more profitable than plenty. The cartel is developed, and neither national good nor the good of human beings takes precedence over the profit of the combination. The cartel and the trust are the logical outgrowth of a competitive economy grounded in self-interest. These are the limitations that organized greed places upon the scientist, the engineer, the social servant of every field, because the economy is based upon the conception not that the self is realized in the gift of self to others but, rather, that the self is realized in taking for the self what it desires.

Why is it that the forces of self-interest fight with all the power at their disposal those measures that seek to bring to all men the very benefits that democracy declares to be its objectives? Self-interest in ownership is met by self-interest in labor, and struggle follows as day the night. Is there no reconciling principle through which the genius of man can be turned from the struggle of man against man to the struggle of man against environment until man masters it, makes the earth fruitful and humanity beautiful? Take the case of the National Resources Planning Board! What forces were responsible for Congressional denial of appropriations? What of the principles that guided the Board? What of the principles written into the Baruch-Hancock report? The following quotations will indicate the seas that separate them. Here is the view of the National Resources Planning Board and its "New Bill of Rights":

> The decisions taken during the war will make possible or impossible the execution of the plans which we as a people make for the peace. We need to see more and more clearly the kind of world toward which we are headed in order to maintain the fighting spirit of our armed forces and the ardor of our industrial workers. We need to stir the imagination and aspirations of all people, free or temporarily enslaved, for new objectives, new goals which can be reached when the war is won. . . .
>
> To win the peace we must call on those deeper resources of the spirit which provide patience and endurance through crisis and which light the future with vision and with hope. . . .
>
> Experience clearly shows that it is impossible to maintain high standards of living without a dynamic economy; that it is impossible to live in peace without some effective force of world concert and order; that only under the fraternal influence of a democratic society can there be any security either for peace or pros-

perity, liberty and justice, or the continuing advancement of the spiritual ideals we cherish above material gains.

This is the inexorable trend of our time, dictated by the growth of human intelligence, and by the awakening nobility of the human spirit with its insistent demand for fraternal recognition and appreciation by fellow men. This upsurging human personality, even in the terrible grip of war, looks for the new heavens and the new earth within its sight and grasp for the first time. If men of good will cannot unite to find a direction and show the way, men of bad will appear; they will loot the ships of state wrecked by the false lights on the shore.

It is for these aims that the United States is striking its hammer blows in this titanic struggle. This is not a war for revenge and conquest; for more lands, and more people; but for a peaceful and fraternal world in which the vast machinery of technology, of organization, of production may be made to serve as the effective instruments of human ideals of liberty and justice. . . .

A NEW BILL OF RIGHTS

1. The right to work, usefully and creatively through the productive years;
2. The right to fair pay, adequate to command the necessities and amenities of life in exchange for work, ideas, thrift, and other socially valuable service;
3. The right to adequate food, clothing, shelter, and medical care;
4. The right to security, with freedom from fear of old age, want, dependency, sickness, unemployment, and accident;
5. The right to live in a system of free enterprise, free from compulsory labor, irresponsible private power, arbitrary public authority, and unregulated monopolies;
6. The right to come and go, to speak or to be silent, free from the spyings of secret political police;
7. The right to equality before the law, with equal access to justice in fact;

8. The right to education, for work, for citizenship, and for personal growth and happiness; and
9. The right to rest, recreation, and adventure, the opportunity to enjoy life and take part in an advancing civilization.[4]

The Baruch *Report on War and Post-War Adjustment Policies* states:

> It is an easier task to convert from peace to war than from war to peace. With the coming of war a sort of totalitarianism is asserted. The Government tells each business what it is to contribute to the war program—just what it is to make and where it is to get the stuff out of which to make it. The planning and execution rest upon one over-all purpose and a single control. Patriotism exercises a strong compulsion.
>
> With peace the opposite becomes true. Each has the right to make what he pleases. Governmental direction and aid disappear. The markets become free and each individual is dependent upon his vision, his courage, his resourcefulness and his energy.[5]

Even though we be unwilling to move from the principle of Jesus to its full practice, it would appear that the necessities of the whole people must take precedence over the exigencies of a part of the people; or, to put it baldly, the self-interest of the group must be paramount and the self-interest of the single individual subordinate. The motive that lives in the minds of those directing the Tennesse Valley Authority is service through which moral ideals may be realized. But even if this were not so, the logic of self-interest would suggest the wisdom of developing all of the resources of the Valley for all. No, self-interest does not work

[4] *National Resources Development Report for 1943* (U. S. Government Printing Office), III, 2, 3.

[5] *Report on War and Post-War Adjustment* ***Policies,*** **February 15, 1944** (U. S. Government Printing Office, 1944), p. 3.

that way for the good reason that the strong will control the weak for themselves. It is only when the strong are driven by the principle of self-realization that their strength is given to the group, or when the group is organized around the principle the Master taught, that the strong must serve all.

Orozco saw the Christ released from the cross. His teaching must be released from the crucifying assumptions that they are not to be practiced. Did Algernon Charles Swinburne see what Orozco saw? Too deep was his understanding of the Lord Christ's heart to accuse him of profanation. He, too, had stood before the crucifix at a wayside shrine, upon his heart the pain of the people and upon his ears their prayers. He dares address the Figure hanging there, even as the thief had spoken on Golgotha long ago:

> God of this grievous people, wrought
>   After the likeness of their race,
> By faces like thine own besought,
>   Thine own blind, helpless, eyeless face,
> I, too, that have nor tongue nor knee
>   For prayer, I have a word to Thee.

Before we condemn the question he dares put, let us remember he had seen "women . . . with gaunt backs bowed by servitude, stop, shift their loads, and pray, and fare forth with souls easier for the prayer." And now he questions:

> It was for this, then, that thy speech
>   Was blown about the world in flame
> And men's souls shot up out of reach
>   Of fear or lust or thwarting shame—
> That thy faith over souls should pass
>   As sea-winds burning the grey grass?

It was for this, that prayers like these
Should spend themselves about thy feet
And with hard, over-labored knees
Kneeling, these slaves of men should beat
Bosoms too lean to suckle sons
And fruitless as their orisons?

It was for this, that men should make
Thy name a fetter on men's necks,
Poor men made poorer for thy sake,
And women withered out of sex.
It was for this, that slaves should be,
Thy word was passed to set men free?

Have we, his followers, consigned the Christ to the tomb, his revolutionary thought wrapped carefully in creedal grave clothes and a great stone of self-interest rolled before the entrance? Are those who would see him to be told he is not here?

It was as a boy that I heard Emma Goldman, the anarchist, inveigh against the Christ—a gospel for slaves, she said. I heard it again in Moscow, when intelligent men who knew only the crucifix Christ, the Christ of ritual, the infant Christ—revolutionaries who had never seen the revolutionary Christ—misread the Beatitudes and beheld in meekness the trait most cherished in the masses by the exploiter, ridiculed turning the other cheek, and laughed at love as a freeing force. "Enslaving is the gospel," they said.

The gift of self is more than intellectual affirmation. It is an act—an act of vital significance in revolution. If the action of the revolution of our time is but the seizure of the privileges of the propertied by the unprivileged propertyless, then possessors are dispossessed and new possessors in the old spirit await the coming of yet another revolution, and man's vaunted progress is but the rushing of the squirrel in the wheel that ever turns but never advances. The classless society will never be established by a class that seeks power for self. It awaits the day when man, seeing the intrinsic practicability of Christ's principle of self-realization, calls for its incarnation in lives that will spend themselves in the action it demands. "Greater love hath no man than this, that a man lay down his life for his friends." Jesus expressed it in the eternal words, "Whosoever would be first among you, shall be servant of all." It is of the essence of his revelation. He who would find his life must lose it.

Paul understood it too. He wrote, "The aim of the Christian discipline is the love that springs from a pure heart, from a good conscience, and from a sincere faith" (Moffatt). All discipline has an objective. Military discipline is for the purpose of imposing one's will upon the enemy through the destruction of his organized forces. Men discipline themselves that they may write with precision and beauty, or successfully pursue truth in research, or capture reality and bring it to men in music, sculpture, painting. For some, the object of discipline is power, for others wealth, and for some the satisfaction of an inner urge to serve and to create. There is the discipline imposed from without, by external will, coercive in nature; there is the discipline developed within by individual will, compelling in spirit. But the aim of Christian discipline is love.

Religious disciplines are many: they are seen in worship, private devotions, and quiet communion as well as in the extreme forms of self-denial and mortification of the flesh. The test of all discipline is this, Does it result in love? "By their fruits ye shall know them." Christian discipline envisages a disciple who has so learned Christ that he loves his brother as Christ loved all his brethren. Christian love is not an abstraction. It springs from a pure heart, a good conscience, and a sincere faith. Love that leaps across the barriers of race and class and nation cannot spring from an emotional life that is immature, nor from a bad conscience. It springs from a sincere faith, a faith in the fact of a moral universe, a basic belief in God, a certainty that this is our Father's world. The aim of discipline is love. It is the love that summons the individual to the realization of self through the complete gift of self to others.

The application of this principle by the great souls of history is sufficient testimony to its validity. I speak not alone of the saints of religion who have placed their hands upon the leper but also of the saints of science who remove the curse of leprosy from the body of man; of those intrepid spirits who have gone to far lands to preach and live the gospel of their Lord; of devoted souls who have gone from library to social struggle that men may be free; of the unbowed and the unconquered who, torn from hearthstone and thrown into concentration camp, have kept their faith; of brothers of conviction who have reached decision in the silent hours of the night, some to bear a prison number because they could not bear arms and some to sleep beneath the rude crosses of a foreign field because they were resolved that freedom should not perish from the earth.

Jesus was not a social reformer. He left no global blueprints, no tax schedules, no five-year plan. But he preached the principles that demand the blueprint and the schedule, the never-ending planning of the moral means whereby the moral ideal becomes real. He gave to the social movement not only an ideal but the Person driven by the spirit essential to the realization of the ideal. The institutions built upon foundations of greed by men of selfishness are doomed. The reformers call for slum clearance, but the revolutionary Jesus calls for the clearing of the souls of men from the spirit of the slum, from the selfishness that breeds disease and disorder, that degrades the person and disgraces the community. He sought no submergence of self in the sea of the community. He called for the highest development of the self, but insisted that the individual never reaches true selfhood until he has dedicated himself to the service of others. Thus the self grows. Greater giving comes from the greater soul. Jesus saw that unlimited growth in the realm of the spirit is possible, but that growth is dependent upon roots in the soil of service and light from the skies of God. Jesus has been called "the fool," and the principle has been termed "magnificent obsession"; but the descriptions do not change the force described. It is a revolutionary force, summoning men to a new way that leads to a new world.

This gift of self is not to be confused with the act of a reckless spendthrift. The command of Jesus was to love thy neighbor as thyself. This is not to think lowly of self. It is to think in the highest terms of self, but to observe that the law of self-growth is the expression of the self in the service of other selves. I heard a brilliant scholar suggest that he once thought the solution of our human problem lay in making clear to all men that they should shift their endeavors from activities that seek possessions to those activities that are creative, because in the former the number of possessions that can be had is limited but the satisfactions in the latter are unlimited. He spoke enthusiastically of the scholar whose search is rewarded by discovery, concluding that discovery is sufficient reward and no acclaim is necessary. But he overlooked an important aspect of the problem. Unless there are other scholars who can share his findings, unless the discovery moves to the service or enrichment of man—in a word, unless penicillin can heal the disease by destroying the attacking bacteria—there is little point to it all; in fact, without society, such discoveries are meaningless. Fortunately, the neighbor is present; and the growth of self in research, in scholarship, in creative writing and invention, finds its true meaning when the products of laboratory and of library are given by the growing self to others. The scientist who gives his finding to his fellows is heralded, and properly so. He has found himself. It does not follow that the soul grows when discovery is patented and kept from the market to protect profitable enterprise it might supplant or controlled by the owner and sold only to those who are able to pay the controlled high price. There are contradictory principles at work here. Jesus preached a rule of conduct that revolutionizes commonly accepted codes. It is the house that is builded on the rock that withstands the storm. The sands of self-interest are unsafe foundations for the house of man.

Long-continued compromise will not do. A bit of new cloth may remain with the old garment for a time; but it is the new garment that is needed, or the rent is made worse. New wine may be held by old bottles for a day, but new bottles are necessary lest the old ones break and the wine run out. When the new wine is poured into new bottles, bottle and wine are preserved.

The love of self and of neighbor, because of man's imperfections, may be less than perfect. Jesus knew this, but he also knew that such love, imperfect though it be, may lose much of its imperfection when related to the absolute love of God. It is God who must be loved with mind and heart and soul, as well as the neighbor. Love of God and love of neighbor, in the heart of a man who wills to love, possess sufficient dynamic to create and keep constant the Christian conduct which the revolutionary principle demands.

In the revolutionary thought of Jesus there is a complete reversal of values. The first are to be the last, and the last first. Is this reversal necessary to bring practice into harmony with moral law? It was not enough to desire right, to mean well, said Jesus; he insisted upon the deed, the righteous act, the cup of cold water. The conflict between the demands of social practice and the commands of conscience must be ended by carrying conscience into the reordering of society, so that society's demand and conscience' command shall be one. This is but to recognize that the sickness of society is moral. The economic paralysis that today affects a hand or a foot will not be cured until the moral blood clot in the brain is absorbed or removed. It is to be remembered that all things are added unto us when we seek *first* the Kingdom of God. It is to recognize that we cannot serve God and mammon. Jesus challenged the immoral axioms of his day, and the challenge in effect was revolution. It was not only a challenge of the immoral axiom but a command to become allegiant to moral principle. He was not interested in directing attention to minute regulations which, if obeyed, would enable man to live on a level of minimum goodness—the amount of goodness, let us say, necessary to pass the guard at the heavenly gate—but rather in summoning all life to the mighty principles which, if sought, would enable men to move to higher and higher levels and approach maximum goodness, the divinity worthy of man. He did not point to page and paragraph in a code of conduct; he turned to the law of love. He did not seek the particular bit of legalism applicable to a particular act. He sought the love that would rally the adventurous to the fellowship of service.

Jesus never identified the particular measure with the absolute he proclaimed. He saw in the measure the expression of the ideal. A man who binds up wounds, carries a brother who has been robbed to an inn and there makes provision for him, is a neighbor. We were commanded to do likewise; but if all the Samaritans were to search out all the Jericho Roads, and all of the robbed were roomed, the gospel would be directing men to greater service—in fact, the fullest expression might call for the gift of life for a friend.

How far can the Golden Rule be applied in competitive struggle? I know there is need for housing, but housing projects may net me only 2 per cent on my investment. There is also the possibility of opening a luxurious cafe which may bring me 15 per cent. Am I to choose the housing proposal or the restaurant? It may be said that the iron laws of the economic sphere will care for that. If too many seek to open restaurants, some will fail; and investors will look elsewhere, eventually getting around to housing. Is there no other motivation by which skilled labor and engineering and architectural ability may be applied to the materials we know how to supply, and with the aid of machines, erect the house? Is there no way whereby the needs of the people may be met by the people's abiltiy to produce? I do not mean to suggest that Jesus was a political revolutionary. Not at all. But the principles he proposed, and the practices he demanded, call for revolutionary change, the jettisoning of much so-called principle, the end of much of present practice. "Ye must be born again." The individual, and society too. Do men find figs on thistles? Are stones fit substitutes for bread? It is a good tree that bringeth forth good fruit. The corrupt tree bringeth forth evil fruit. Such trees are cut down and cast into the fire. This is revolutionary preaching.

This is not the day of the monastery. It is the day of the mine, the mill, the market place. Solace cannot be found in separation. If Christianity cannot bring the machine to Christ, as well as man to Christ, men will turn with machine and material to others who would be saviors. No, the machine cannot accept Christ. But Christ can accept the machine.

The revolutionary Christ preached a principle, called for a practice, but more, he revealed in his person the principle and the practice. It was his own life he gave. He did not assign to Peter the task of washing the disciples' feet, to James the agony in Gethsemane's darkness, nor to John death upon the Cross. It was he who took the basin and the towel. It was he who prayed, "Not my will, but thine, be done." It was he who whispered, "Into thy hands I commend my spirit."

It is well-nigh sacrilege to suggest an Upper Room in which the Leader called for a volunteer to bear the cross, or even that lots be cast to determine the disciple who should die. He knew that when he broke the bread and gave them the wine to drink that the symbols spoke of his own body and his own blood. Salvation awaits the gamblers unafraid who are ready to throw their lives for a world redeemed.

Jesus was a revolutionary who preached the absolute, who dared to say, "Be ye therefore Perfect." This he said to sinful men. He was a revolutionary who knew that man does not live by bread alone but who prayed first, "Give us this day our daily bread." Man's life does not consist in the abundance of the things he possesses, he said; but he condemned the pious who would devour widow's houses. He saw that life is not food and raiment; but the righteous, who are to inherit eternal life, are those about whom he could say, "I was hungry, and ye gave me to eat, . . . naked, and ye clothed me." His clothes had been stripped from his body. He had suffered the indignity of the scarlet robe. He was the revolutionary never indifferent to the necessities but resolved that the externals must minister to the essentials. He knew the heart of man. Revolution must do more than build a house; it must change the heart. He forgave the woman of the streets and accepted an alabaster box from a prostitute; but the Son of God who was also Son of Man knew that the prostitution of the body of a woman was more than the violation of an ancient command, "Thou shalt not commit adultery." It was first the desire of one who "looketh on a woman to lust after her," for he "hath committed adultery with her already in his heart." Jesus knew that much long prayer was pretense. He knew, too, that the stumbling petition of a sinner might spring from a sincere heart. He was a revolutionary. He believed his teaching and thrust his life forward upon his convictions. "In him was life; and the life was the light of men. And the light shineth in darkness; and the darkness comprehended it not"—"the darkness has never overpowered it."

Ten years ago, when in Oxford, I noted that the students were to present a new play by John Masefield. The poet laureate was announced to speak. It turned out that he was not only playwright but stage director, friend of the players, speaker of the evening. The play itself concluded with the reading of a benediction. It was as though a voice had spoken from the sacred pages of yesterday. I wrote Mr. Masefield requesting a copy. He replied that he had dashed off the lines during the course of the play and that the one who read them had taken the bit of paper away. I was disappointed. Later, to my delight and very great appreciation, I received another letter from Mr. Masefield, in which he said he had found the lines and was happy to share them. And now, remembering that it was said of Christ "In him was life; and the life was the light of men," I conclude with the Masefield benediction:

> Light comfort you, Light gladden you, Light bless you,
> Light fill your heart, and through you lighten the world.

THE LYMAN BEECHER LECTURES ON PREACHING [1]

YALE UNIVERSITY DIVINITY SCHOOL

Established May 2, 1872, by Mr. Henry W. Sage in honor of Rev. Lyman Beecher, D.D.

1871-1872 Henry Ward Beecher, *Yale Lecturer on Preaching,* first series, New York, J. B. Ford & Co., 1872.

1872-1873 Henry Ward Beecher, *Yale Lectures on Preaching,* second series, New York, J. B. Ford & Co., 1873.

1873-1874 Henry Ward Beecher, *Yale Lectures on Preaching,* third series, New York, J. B. Ford & Co., 1874. A one-volume edition, *Yale Lectures on Preaching,* was published by The Pilgrim Press, Chicago.

1874-1875 John Hall, *God's Word Through Preaching,* New York, Dodd & Mead, 1875.

1875-1876 William Mackergo Taylor, *The Ministry of the Word,* New York, Anson D. F. Randolph & Co., 1876.

1876-1877 Phillips Brooks, *Lectures on Preaching,* New York, E. P. Dutton & Co., 1877.

1877-1878 Robert William Dale, *Nine Lectures on Preaching,* New York, A. S. Barnes & Co., 1878.

1878-1879 Matthew Simpson, *Lectures on Preaching,* New York, Nelson & Philips, 1879.

1879-1880 Howard Crosby, *The Christian Preacher,* New York, Anson D. F. Randolph & Co., 1880.

[1] Compiled by Rev. Hal Earl Norton, D.D., Pastor, The Roundy Memorial Baptist Church, Milwaukee, Wisconsin.

1880-1881 Joseph Tuthill Duryea, George Harris, Samuel E. Herrick, Nathaniel Judson Burton, and Llewelyn David Bevan. Lectures not published.

1881-1882 Ezekiel Gilman Robinson, *Lectures on Preaching,* New York, Henry Holt & Co., 1883.

1882-1883 No lectures.

1883-1884 Nathaniel Judson Burton, *Yale Lectures on Preaching and Other Writings,* The Pilgrim Press, 1887. Reprinted by The Macmillan Co., 1925, under the title *In Pulpit and Parish.*

1884-1885 Henry Martin Storrs, *The American Preacher.* Not published.

1885-1886 William Mackergo Taylor, *The Scottish Pulpit,* New York, Harper & Bros., 1887.

1886-1887 Washington Gladden, *Tools and the Man,* Boston, Houghton Mifflin Co., 1893.

1887-1888 Henry Clay Trumbull, *The Sunday School,* Philadelphia, John P. Wattles, 1888.

1888-1899 John Albert Broadus, *Preparation and Delivery of Sermons,* New York, Harper & Bros., 1897.

1889-1890 Adolphus Julius Frederick Behrends, *The Philosophy of Preaching,* New York, Charles Scribner's Sons, 1893.

1890-1891 James Stalker, *The Preacher and His Models,* New York, A. C. Armstrong, 1893.

1891-1892 Andrew Martin Fairbairn, *The Place of Christ in Modern Theology,* New York, Charles Scribner's Sons, 1893.

1892-1893 Robert Foreman Horton, *Verbum Dei,* New York, The Macmillan Co., 1893.

1893-1894 No lectures.

1894-1895 David Hummell Greer, *The Preacher and His Place,* New York, Charles Scribner's Sons, 1895.

1895-1896 Henry van Dyke, *The Gospel for an Age of Doubt,* New York, The Macmillan Co., 1896.

1896-1897 John Watson (Ian Maclaren), *The Cure of Souls,* New York, Dodd & Mead, 1896.

1897-1898 William Jewett Tucker, *The Making and the Unmaking of the Preacher,* Boston, Houghton Mifflin Co., 1898.

1898-1899 Sir George Adam Smith, *Modern Criticism and the Preaching of the Old Testament,* New York, A. C. Armstrong, 1901.

1899-1900 John Brown, *Puritan Preaching in England,* New York, Charles Scribner's Sons, 1900.

1900-1901 No lectures.

1901-1902 Washington Gladden, *Social Salvation,* Boston, Houghton Mifflin Co., 1902.

1902-1903 George Angier Gordon, *Ultimate Conceptions of Faith,* Boston, Houghton Mifflin Co., 1903.

1903-1904 Lyman Abbott, *The Christian Ministry,* Boston, Houghton Mifflin Co., 1905.

1904-1905 Francis Greenwood Peabody, *Jesus Christ and the Christian Character,* New York, The Macmillan Co., 1908.

1905-1906 Charles Reynolds Brown, *The Social Message of the Modern Pulpit,* New York, Charles Scribner's Sons, 1906.

1906-1907 Peter Taylor Forsyth, *Positive Preaching and the Modern Mind,* London, Hodder & Stoughton, 1907.

1907-1908 William Herbert Perry Faunce, *The Educational Ideal in the Ministry,* New York, The Macmillan Co., 1908; reprinted 1919.

1908-1909 Herbert Hensley Hensen, *The Liberty of Prophesying,* New Haven, Yale University Press, 1910.

1909-1910 Charles Edward Jefferson, *The Building of the Church,* New York, The Macmillan Co., 1910.

1910-1911 Frank Wakeley Gunsaulus, *The Minister and the Spiritual Life,* New York, Fleming H. Revell, 1911.

1911-1912 John Henry Jowett, *The Preacher: His Life and Work,* New York, George H. Doran, 1912.

1912-1913 Charles Henry Parkhurst, *The Pulpit and the Pew,* New Haven, Yale University Press, 1913.

1913-1914 Charles Sylvester Horne, *The Romance of Preaching,* New York, Fleming H. Revell, 1914.
1914-1915 George Wharton Pepper, *A Voice from the Crowd,* New Haven, Yale University Press, 1915.
1915-1916 William DeWitt Hyde, *The Gospel of Good Will,* New York, The Macmillan Co., 1916.
1916-1917 William Fraser McDowell, *Good Ministers of Jesus Christ,* New York, The Abingdon Press, 1917.
1917-1918 Henry Sloane Coffin, *In a Day of Social Rebuilding,* New Haven, Yale University Press, 1918.
1918-1919 John Kelman, *The War and Preaching,* New Haven, Yale University Press, 1919.
1919-1920 Albert Parker Fitch, *Preaching and Paganism,* New Haven, Yale University Press, 1920.
1920-1921 Charles David Williams, *The Prophetic Ministry for* Today, New York, The Macmillan Co., 1921.
1921-1922 William Pierson Merrill, *The Freedom of the Preacher,* New York, The Macmillan Co., 1922.
1922-1923 Charles Reynolds Brown, *The Art of Preaching,* New York, The Macmillan Co., 1922.
1923-1924 Harry Emerson Fosdick, *The Modern Use of the Bible,* New York, The Macmillan Co., 1924.
1924-1925 William Ralph Inge, *The Preaching of the Kingdom of God in History.* Lectures not published.
1925-1926 Raymond Calkins, *The Eloquence of the Christian Experience,* New York, The Macmillan Co., 1927.
1926-1927 John Robert Paterson Sclater, *The Public Worship of God,* New York, Doubleday, Doran & Co., 1927.
1927-1928 James Edward Freeman, *The Ambassador,* New York, The Macmillan Co., 1928.
1928-1929 Edwin Du Bose Mouzon, *Preaching with Authority,* New York, The Macmillan Co., 1929.
1929-1930 Francis John McConnell, *The Prophetic Ministry,* New York, The Abingdon Press, 1930.
1930-1931 George Arthur Buttrick, *Jesus Came Preaching,* New York, Charles Scribner's Sons, 1931.

1931-1932 Ernest Fremont Tittle, *Jesus After Nineteen Centuries*, New York, The Abingdon Press, 1932.

1932-1933 Lawrence Pearsall Jacks, *Elemental Religion*, New York, Harper & Bros., 1934.

1933-1934 Albert Edward Day, *Jesus and Human Personality*, New York, The Abingdon Press, 1934.

1934-1935 Walter Russell Bowie, *The Renewing Gospels*, New York, Charles Scribner's Sons, 1935.

1935-1936 John Edgar Park, *The Miracle of Preaching*, New York, The Macmillan Co., 1936.

1936-1937 No lectures.

1937-1938 Willard Learoyd Sperry, *We Prophesy in Part*, New York, Harper & Bros., 1938.

1938-1939 Charles Clayton Morrison, *What Is Christianity?* Chicago, Willett, Clark & Co., 1940.

1939-1940 George Arthur Buttrick, Edwin McNeill Poteat, Arthur Howe Bradford, Elmore McNeill McKee, Wyatt Aiken Smart, and Ernest Fremont Tittle, *Preaching in These Times*. New York, Charles Scribner's Sons, 1940.

1940-1941 Ralph Washington Sockman, *The Highway of God*, New York, The Macmillan Company, 1942.

1941-1942 Morgan Phelps Noyes, *Preaching the Word of God*, New York, Charles Scribner's Sons, 1943.

1942-1943 Paul Scherer, *For We Have This Treasure*, New York, Harper & Bros., 1944.

1943-1944 G. Bromley Oxnam, *Preaching in a Revolutionary Age*, New York and Nashville, Abingdon-Cokesbury Press, 1944.